MY GOD WILL SUPPLY

HOW THE LORD
PROVIDES IN
TIMES OF
SHORTAGE

MY GOD WILL SUPPLY

DEDE ROBERTSON
with John Sherrill

Published by

Lincoln, Virginia 22078

Distributed by Word Books • Waco, Texas 76703

Library of Congress Cataloging in Publication Data

Robertson, Dede.
  My God will supply.

  1. Robertson, Dede. 2. Christian biography—
United States. 3. Soybean as food. 4. Cookery
(Soybeans) I. Sherrill, John, joint author.
II. Title.
BR1725.R616A35   248′.2 [B]   79–16126

ISBN 0–912376–48–1

LET THE READER
BE WARNED

WHEN MY HUSBAND Pat learned that I planned to include my Dream in a book about God's supply, he was intrigued.

And worried.

"I can see why you include dreams as part of God's provision, Dede," Pat said. "That's perfectly Biblical.

"But," he went on, "I think you ought also to include a caveat in your book." Pat has a law degree and *caveat* is lawyer language meaning *warning.* "You're not claiming this Dream is prophetic, you're only suggesting that it *might* be. I'll admit your Dream is intriguing. Especially since some of the details appear to be coming true. But so far that's all that has happened. The Dream has partially come to pass.

"But we just cannot jump from there to assume there'll be an atomic disaster. We've got to be careful to weigh all possible 'words from the Lord.' Check them out against Scripture. Listen to the witness of our own spirits. Ask ourselves if the word is consistent with God's revealed plan.

"But if—just *if*—the Dream is God speaking to us in the way He spoke to His people so often in the Bible, then your book takes on an incredible importance, one that is heartwarming and encouraging. Because in it you are sharing what we have been learning about God's provision for His people, when provision seems impossible."

Dede Robertson

INTRODUCTION

AT ONE LEVEL this is a book about soybeans. At another level it is a book about God's protection. The two are directly related.

When Pat wrote *Shout It from the Housetops* with Jamie Buckingham, they included a chapter called "Thank God for Soybeans." One day on the "700 Club," the talk show and intercessory prayer time which is the heart of the Christian Broadcasting Network, I found myself speaking about Pat's and my long interest in the soybean.

Pat mentioned this interest on the show several times as well. People from all over the country began to write, asking me to tell them about my soybeans and asking me to share with them the best of my recipes. My favorites—each named for one of the Fruit of the Spirit—are included in this book on God's supply.

At the same time, Pat and I received an impressive number of letters from listeners saying that they wanted to hear about the events that led up to the founding of CBN—not from Pat's viewpoint but from my own. These correspondents were sure that, although Pat and I lived through the same events, we would see them from different perspectives, and from them find different light.

"Please, Dede," I heard time and again, "do tell us more about what the Lord has been teaching *you* in these adventures."

So I have tried to make this a helpful book. I want especially to emphasize God's provision, both physical and spiritual. But I have tried to make this a fun book, too, by telling of my romance with the soybean. Throughout, the story of God's provision and the tale of our encounters with the soybean are one and the same story. The Lord has taught me so much about Himself through the humble little bean!

I find what He says encouraging.

I hope you will too.

Dede

ACKNOWLEDGMENTS

John Sherrill and I would like to express our special thanks to Phil March, Miji Teichmann and Rita Watson for their generous help in the preparation of this manuscript.

LOVE WAFFLES

This is far and away my family's favorite soybean dish. Even our son Tim likes "Love Waffles."

1 cup unbleached flour (or ¾ cup flour and ¼ cup wheat germ)
1 cup soybeans, soaked and cooked, then either ground or blended
2 t baking powder, combination type
½ t salt
1 T sugar
3 egg yolks, beaten (put aside the whites)
5 T salad oil or melted butter
1½ cups milk

Heat the waffle iron. Iron is ready when a drop of water forms a small ball. If water sizzles, iron is too hot.

Mix ingredients together with a few swift strokes—like muffin batter. Beat 3 egg whites until stiff, not dry. Fold egg whites into batter until they are barely blended. Bake on waffle iron until done. These are very good served with maple syrup, orange syrup, strawberry preserves or fresh fruit.

If you have sour milk or sour cream, use 2 eggs instead of 3, and then use 1½ t baking powder and ¼ t baking soda.
Yield: Six Waffles

MARRIAGE IS SUPPOSED to be a fairy tale, isn't it? You meet the man of your dreams and marry him. Then you live happily ever after. When I was a little girl living in Ohio I never gave much thought to married life following any other pattern. I just knew that some day I would meet a man who would be interesting and fun . . . and tall. He absolutely had to be tall, because I stood five feet six inches myself in my stocking feet.

With my Prince Charming I would become a gracious lady. We would live somewhere in South America, perhaps in a villa built around an open courtyard filled with fountains and flowers.

We would have a nursemaid, of course, to take care of our three or four children, to bathe them at night and put them to bed. I would then read the children stories and tell them tales of bunny rabbits and dancing bears and little princesses. When dinner was served on the patio by maids and butlers my husband would smile at me through the flickering candles that graced our table. Life would go on like this forever.

11

I sometimes wonder where such romantic thoughts came from. At first glance they certainly weren't evident in my practical, down-to-earth parents and grandparents. Daddy's grandfather was from early settler stock, a Vermont farmer with seven daughters. That's a combination that calls for a lot of realism. Great-grandfather Perry displayed his practical nature by moving away from the rock-bound Vermont farm to start a pie-baking business in Ohio. I still have a photograph of an old horse-drawn wagon that was used to sell his wares door to door. There on the side of one of the wagons were the words, printed proudly, *Perry's Pies.*

But then a romantic streak showed up in the family make-up. Great-grandfather Perry grew tired of the pie business even though it was a success and moved *back* to his beloved, if rock-bound, Vermont. There he found seven husbands for his seven daughters. One of the daughters, Wilhelmina, married a man named Fred Elmer. And the two headed once again back to Ohio, where they took up baking pies in the still thriving family business.

So there was a mixture of the fanciful and of the downright pragmatic in my blood. I bring that up because at first, frankly, I was inclined to think of my "Secret Dream" as belonging to the former category. Just an overactive imagination at work.

Now I'm not so sure.

The dream occurred while I was still in college, living at home in Columbus, Ohio. There was nothing unusual about the circumstances surrounding the dream. Daddy was about his daily routines, rising early in the morning to fix breakfast before Mother got up, then taking off for his work as general manager of the Hanna Paint Manufacturing Company. Our Tudor house in the suburbs of

Columbus was so solid and typical that nothing mystic or prophetic seemed at all in place there. It sat back comfortably from the road, had a lot of old trees around it, boasted a pleasant, well-cared-for lawn.

Yet it was in my room on the second floor of this house that the dream occurred.

That night I went to bed just as I always did in the company of my blue-and-white statue to the Virgin Mary sitting serenely on the mantle over the fireplace in my room. There was a holy-water font, complete with ceramic angel, at the door of my room too. Because of these touches some people thought of me as the religious member of the household. Actually I was just going through the motions. My real religious attitudes could perhaps best be summed up with the little doggerel we schoolgirls liked to quote:

> Blessed St. Anthony
> Dear St. Ann
> Send me a man
> As fast as you can.

Mother, I think, understood that there wasn't much substance to my devotions. She was, for those days, an unusual Roman Catholic. She didn't agree with any emphasis on the Virgin Mary but put her own emphasis on the Bible. How often I saw her sitting in her favorite chair in the living room reading Scripture!

Nor was there anything dramatic going on in my own life, which was in fact quite gay and happy. There was no serious crisis. No health problem. No unusual trouble at school. Nothing at all that could have pointed to a psychological explanation of the dream. Yet that night . . .

I woke up.

Never had I experienced anything even remotely like this dream.

> *I was in a room in a large country house. I was standing at the window looking out over a lake. There were pine trees nearby. With me in the room was a man. With me also were three or four other people. I had met none of them in real life, yet I knew that they were close to me and were important to me.*
>
> *Suddenly the scene became ominously, strangely still. I heard a motor. I looked out the window and saw something like a parachute coming down from the sky. An object dangled from the end of the shroud lines beneath the canopy. I called to the man and the other people to come look. Something about the scene frightened us all. The man urged us to head for the basement.*
>
> *We all tumbled down a set of steep steps into the cellar and closed the door, whereupon there was an explosion. We could not see it, but we could hear it and feel it. The lights went out. We were all very confused. Something of vast significance had taken place. We had lived through it.*
>
> *There was some food and water in the cellar so we stayed there for several days. Finally we felt it was safe to go see what had happened. As we crept up the steep stairs and opened the cellar door the thing that struck us was the silence. There wasn't a sound anywhere. We climbed out to a scene of vast desolation. Everything we knew was gone, burned up. The country house was in ruins around us. The trees, the grass, were all brown.*

Then I woke up.

I did not sleep much for the rest of that night for sure! As soon as I heard Daddy stirring about in the kitchen I went down to join him, fully intending to tell him about the dream.

Yet, that morning, there in the sunny comfort of our kitchen, with my hard-working, practical, always-cheerful father puttering about happily, it was suddenly impossible to talk about the dream. What would I say? What would

Daddy say? That I had had a nightmare? Yet in some strange way it wasn't a nightmare because we had all come through the experience safely.

So in the end I ate a bowl of cereal.

And that was all there was to the experience.

Or so I thought.

My childhood was spent in a deeply entrenched Republican atmosphere. (My grandfather Elmer, the one who moved his family *back* to Ohio from Vermont, became a state senator.) I had no way of knowing that the young man I was eventually to marry was growing up at this time in an atmosphere of equally entrenched Virginia Democrats.

Pat and I met in graduate school. With more than a little trepedation I had announced to my parents that I wanted to become a registered nurse. I know what prompted my father's hesitation. He was remembering me as the girl who loved parties, who was always in the center of things whether it was organizing a theater outing or a bridge game or planning a dinner at a swank restaurant or designing homecoming floats at college. He was remembering the girl who liked attention so much that she did crazy things to get it, like allowing herself to be "kidnapped" from her sorority house and carried aloft to the roof of Sigma Chi. It didn't make much sense to Daddy that I wanted to become a nurse. He was certain that I was too weak in the stomach to stand the sight of suffering. But he and Mother eventually yielded to my determination, and in 1952 I entered the graduate studies program at Yale University.

Our dormitory was a grand old mansion just a few blocks from the hospital where I worked when I wasn't in class. The mansion had been renovated so tastefully that it still retained the flavor of its elegant past. The first floor living room was large, with dark floors and tall windows outlined by red draperies. Overstuffed furniture was grouped about the room, inviting quiet chats. The house even boasted small rooms we called date parlors where we could visit with young men.

It was here in this house that I met the man of my storybook dreams. Shortly after I settled into the nursing schedule, it was announced that we would be having a dance and open house. We invited the law school students to join us for the evening.

The whole dorm seemed to come alive as all 60 of us prepared for the event. The dancing would be on the main floor and the refreshment table would be set up downstairs.

Just before the men arrived we plumped up the cushions and turned down the lighting. The hi-fi began to play. We opened the windows so that the cool autumn breeze could carry the music throughout the house. There was a golden aura to the moment. The reds in the chairs, carpets and curtains gave the room a tingle of excitement. It was a night made for dreamers with only one drawback, which my roommate put into words.

"Dede," she whispered as the future lawyers began filling the room, "either we're too tall or they're too short."

"I know," I answered, "Maybe next time we should invite the football squad!"

Just then a short, blond young man caught my eye and smiled. He started toward us. "Good luck," whispered my roommate, turning away.

"Thanks a lot," I whispered back, unable now to avoid the invitation to dance.

And so it went, all evening. To think that I'd spent all that time fixing my shoulder-length hair. I had borrowed a full, peacock blue, felt skirt to wear with my white, crocheted sweater. My best strand of pearls was at my neck and I was feeling quite like a lady.

I noticed the blond boy edging his way towards me again. What could I do? I really wanted to avoid him, not only because I had to talk over the top of his head, but also because he was not at all interesting. "Refreshments!" I thought to myself. "That's it. I'll go downstairs to the refreshment table and try to look busy."

I pardon-me'd my way through the dancing couples and sailed downstairs. The refreshment table was neatly set up with plates of creamy fresh pastries, tiny squares of pastel pink-and-green petit fours, and yellow butter cookies. There were several punch bowls, and couples were standing around helping themselves. Then I noticed the candles. No one had lit the candles yet. That is what I would do.

I heard footsteps on the old wooden stairs. *It's the blond boy, I just know it. I'm going to make myself busy.* I struck a match, pretending not to notice anyone. I lit the near candles first, then leaned over them to reach the ones at the back of the table. And then I stopped abruptly at a peculiar smell. Burning hair! Mine!

Suddenly, a pair of hands were patting my head. And a deep voice said, "Don't worry, it's only singed. It would be too bad to burn that hair."

I turned around and stared. It was not—thank heavens—the boring blond.

"Thank you," I muttered. Who was *this* new dark-haired visitor with the bushy eyebrows and the twinkling eyes! "My name is Dede Elmer."

"And I'm Pat Robertson."

I stared at him a moment. *Pat Robertson,* I said the name over in my mind as I stood looking up at him.

Yes, *up*. Into the blue eyes of the dark-haired gentleman who towered near me. "Would you care to join me for a dance?" he asked.

"Why, of course."

And so as we waltzed around the floor I came to know a bit about Pat Robertson, a man who was not only tall but interesting and fun as well.

Pat was a graduate of Washington and Lee University in Virginia. After his Marine Corps tour of duty in Korea, he came to Yale to study law. What he didn't tell me that evening was that his father was A. Willis Robertson, the United States Senator from Virginia who was chairman of the Banking and Currency Committee.

"Would you care to take a walk?" Pat was asking me. Hand in hand we walked through the big old doorway and onto the campus, laughing quietly as we talked. The music from the open windows seemed to follow us down the block, then faded into the star-filled sky.

In those days about the only place to go for an inexpensive visit was the beer parlor. Which is where we did go for our first date. There were many more dates after that evening. Over the next months we realized that we were falling in love and we began talking about marriage. But when in fact we did marry, it was secretly. We slipped away for a quiet ceremony, not telling our parents because we were quite sure that neither family would approve. Among other reasons, we were still in school and had religious differences.

But our subterfuge didn't work for long. Our first baby was soon on the way, and we had to let our parents know we had married months before. Those were hectic days, made all the more busy by the arrival on November 6, 1954, of our Timmy. That year was one big treadmill of work, shared babysitting, hospital rounds, study, more study made triply difficult with the new baby. I don't know how we ever managed, because there wasn't time to think.

Even before graduation Pat accepted an excellent job with the W. R. Grace conglomerate. In June 1955, when he received his law degree, he was moved to New York City. Until my own graduation I had to stay in New Haven five days a week, but for "our two days" we set up housekeeping in a stone and stucco gatekeeper's cottage on Staten Island, one of the boroughs of New York City.

Then one day, a year after Tim was born, I looked around our tiny cottage where we lived full time now, and realized with amusement that this wasn't exactly my dream come true. There was no butler here. There was no nursemaid. There was no open courtyard or veranda in this gatekeeper's cottage.

Our home consisted of a tiny, one-bedroom cottage. Even the color scheme made the house seem small. The walls were a dark copper and the trim was charcoal and white. The furniture was nondescript except for its color which was also charcoal. The only real brightness in the room came from a huge orange and red painting of a Modigliani nude that hung over the sofa.

I smiled, too, at the realization that my life was no more glamorous than our house. I was alone from early morning until late at night. Like thousands of other young mothers, my days consisted of folding diapers and feeding the baby and cooking meals. I had a degree in nursing, but what good was that doing now?

I did have the consolation of enjoying Timmy. It was a pleasure watching this year-old child, so full of life, becoming aware of his world. It was a world of peek-a-boo and pull toys, reading picture books and sharing lots of laughter. Tim was such a happy child and I was glad to enjoy him alone while I could. Around Christmas of 1955 I began to realize that there was going to be another baby in this world of ours.

It was right at this time that a life-changing event took place in our lives.

For months Pat had been restless. So much so that he quit his secure job with W. R. Grace and went into the electronic components business with some friends from Yale. Still he was unsettled; he couldn't even sit still for long. In our copper-colored living room he was forever getting up and down, playing with Tim for a minute then pouring himself a glass of beer then asking me how I felt, whether the new pregnancy was making me sick . . . a question he had just asked ten minutes before.

Pat's mother phoned one evening and I could tell from Pat's side of the conversation that she was telling him once again that God had a plan for him. Pat sipped his beer and agreed, because it was the easiest thing to do. But I knew that neither he nor I really believed in this kind of Christianity, where God had plans for people. We both considered ourselves to be Christians, but our faith didn't *matter* very much. We simply knew that God existed. Pat's mother, with her letters, tracts, books and phone calls . . . well, it was nice of her to care, but the emphasis on religion frankly bothered me.

Then one night in May 1956, when I was in my sixth month of pregnancy, Pat came into our cottage, all excited. He stood in front of the Modigliani, his blue eyes twinkling more than ever before. He even seemed to stand taller. He moved, almost danced around the room. "Dede," he said, "I have found the Lord."

I stared at him, not believing my ears. "Aren't you being a bit presumptuous, Pat?" This really was an amazing turn of events. I knew that Pat had made a dinner date with some Dutchman who was an evangelist. But "finding the Lord" . . . this was hard to grasp.

"Dede," Pat went on, paying no attention to my protest, "I've been saved! I just know our lives are going to change." What had come over him? What was he talking about?

Well, after that Pat and I argued all the time about this new relationship with Jesus. I'd known Jesus all my life, hadn't I? And so had Pat, hadn't he? Pat started reading the Bible every day. The only other person I knew who read Scripture so regularly was my mother, but she didn't carry her Christianity out as far as Pat! I really began to worry when Pat told me he thought he was being guided to sell out his interests in the electronic components business, which seemed to hold so much promise, and begin to study for the ministry.

Pat was absolutely serious. He came home one day in early June, 1956, with the news that he would be leaving for a month-long summer study program in Canada to prepare him for seminary.

"You are going *where?*"

"Now, Dede, I know you're upset, but this is part of God's plan."

"Pat, look at me," I said, laughing. "I am expecting another baby in just a few weeks. Not only that but we have to move out of this house. Our lease is about up! Remember?"

"I'm sorry, Dede. I know the timing isn't perfect, but this is something that I have to do."

A few days later Pat took off for Canada. I was no longer laughing. I really wanted to pack everything up and go back to Ohio. But I couldn't even do that. When my father retired from his position as executive director of the Hanna Paint Manufacturing business, he and Mother moved overseas, to Lebanon, where he opened a new paint manufacturing business, the Sipes International Paint Company. My brother, Ralph, and his wife, Ginny, had their own lives to lead. So I was really stranded.

Pat arrived back home from Canada in time for the birth of our second child, Elizabeth, on August 14, 1956. But he still had no definite plans. My mother had come all the way from Lebanon to be with me when Elizabeth was born. She kept reminding us that it was ridiculous for Pat to have two degrees and no paying job. To which I could only add a hearty "amen!"

In the fall of 1956, Pat applied for admission to Biblical Seminary in New York. He was accepted and soon after, to get practical training, he was assigned to the Bayside Community Methodist Church as assistant pastor.

So at least Pat was settled. We found a new home, too. The second floor apartment was in Queens, halfway between Biblical Seminary and Pat's new church. There were two bedrooms, a living room, a dining area, kitchen and bath. When a visitor came into the apartment there was no doubt that we had children! Stepping into the foyer, he had to skirt the lineup—a baby carriage, a tricycle, a hobby horse and a shopping cart. The living room was a playroom by day, and by night a place where grownups could sit and chat. On the wall a conservative Van Gogh replaced the orange and red nude of our Staten Island days. The colors in the painting were blue and yellow which echoed the colors of our furniture. I especially liked our living room late at night when it was softly lit by a fluorescent bulb in the fishtank on top of the bookcase, where guppies and angelfish drifted about peacefully.

It would have been a satisfying time for me, except for one problem which I shared with other seminary wives: during the winter of 1956 and into the spring of 1957 I almost never saw my hardworking student husband. It was so bad that I agreed to become a counselor at a Billy Graham crusade in New York, not because I felt I could really counsel people about Jesus, but because I'd be with Pat during the orientation sessions.

Shortly afterwards, in the late spring of 1957, one of those terrible experiences occurred which left me weakened, dispirited and certainly in need of strength outside my own.

One day while Pat was away I began to show symptoms of miscarrying. The doctor ordered me to bed, which wasn't easy with two very young children in the house. Two-and-a-half-year old Tim did his best to help. I talked him through just how to make a peanut butter and jelly sandwich. Then when Pat came home he had to take on all the work I could not do. Poor man, he was suddenly called upon to do five jobs at once: student, pastor, husband, father, and now . . . housekeeper. He had to cook the meals, wash the diapers. I must say that although it hadn't been easy to live with this extremely busy man, when I was in trouble Pat was right beside me.

But in spite of everything I lost the baby. Pat and I were both crushed by the experience. For a while it brought us closer together. But then inevitably, as I began to regain my strength, Pat started once again to study and work pretty much around the clock. The fact that other students were struggling just as hard and were separated just as much was very little consolation. We all missed our husbands!

So, as many wives do in these circumstances, I began to wonder if I shouldn't go to work myself. We needed the money, true. But it was more than that. I needed the companionship of adult men and women, working on a common task. So I began talking with Pat about taking a nursing job.

Immediately this caused friction between us. Pat did not want me to work because he felt it would be bad for Tim and Elizabeth. My mother disagreed. She told me emphatically in her letters that we were living in a new day. It was *better* for the marriage (and consequently for the children) if I went my way and Pat went his way. It sounded logical. I'd walk parallel to my husband, but I wouldn't let him dictate to me.

There was a hospital within a short distance of our apartment so I applied for work and was hired on the spot. I took the 3 to 11 P.M. shift, counting on Pat to be home early enough to relieve the sitter. But time and again when I returned to the apartment just after eleven the sitter was still there because Pat hadn't come in yet. It was hard to say who was more annoyed by education's demands, me or the baby sitter. I tried to suppress my feelings in front of the children, but little Elizabeth became so sensitive that she would begin to cry the moment she saw me put on my white uniform.

One night after once again finding the sitter at home instead of Pat, I just sat up reading, waiting for him.

I was nearly asleep on the sofa when I heard footsteps. Slowly they dragged their way through the hall. Pat fumbled for his keys. They fell. I heard the key in the lock. Pat walked in and mumbled. He was too tired to notice that I had stayed up. Was this the man I married?

"Nice to see you, Pat," I said.

"Hum-yes, yes, Dede." He fell onto the sofa.

"What was it tonight, Pat?"

"What's wrong, Dede?" Pat asked, perplexed.

"What's wrong? Look at you, Pat. You're a wreck. Can't you see what you're doing to your own body?"

Suddenly I realized I was speaking to a sleeping man.

I sighed, kissed him and went to sleep myself, wondering how our marriage would survive the summer.

Something close to bitterness began to creep into my feelings toward Pat. I began to needle him. On Sunday mornings he had to get ready for his Sunday School class at church. Tim was a very early riser, but Pat was awake before him. He went out to the kitchen before six, made coffee and seated himself in the maple-armed Early American chair where he prepared his lesson. In my mind, during those days I did all the work. And I never let Pat forget it. As I prepared breakfast and cleaned up after the children it was with a supply of groans and sarcastic remarks, like, "Why don't you practice your Christianity, Pat, instead of burying your head in a Bible? I need some help here."

There probably was *some* reason to be resentful but not nearly as much as I thought. I'm afraid I deliberately set out to destroy the gains I could see in Pat's spiritual life by trying to get him mad. And when I couldn't succeed, I grew depressed instead, banging pots and scolding Tim and wondering how long I could take life as the wife of a man who talked in born-again language, and worse still tried to get me to admit that I needed an experience like the one he had.

Then God intervened. In the late summer of 1957 Pat's mother offered to pay our expenses to take a vacation. We chose a Bible camp, partly because it was inexpensive. Pat signed up at the Word of Life Inn at Schroon Lake in upstate New York.

I was pleasantly surprised by the setting. There was a large, white inn overlooking a lake, with smaller buildings scattered about in the woods.

One night a man named Larry McGuill was speaking. Pat offered to babysit if I wanted to go. I thought I sensed a ploy on his part, but I accepted nevertheless because it meant getting out for a few hours.

That night at seven-thirty I was sitting in the audito-

rium—toward the back as usual—listening to Larry speak
about hardening our hearts. Another of those evangelical
terms! But I sort of knew what he meant. He was saying
that I had my heart set against yielding my life to Jesus.
Well, perhaps he was right. But was it necessary to make
a public confession? I just didn't see the need for anything
quite so personal. Was that hard heartedness?

"Yes."

It was as if a word had been spoken inside me. A warm
and gentle word, at once encouraging and challenging.
It wasn't that as a Catholic I couldn't find a personal
life with Jesus; it was, rather, that I *had* not done so.
And right now, sitting there in the rear of the auditorium
at Schroon Lake, I was hardening my heart.

"Jesus is knocking," Larry was saying. But it wasn't
Larry speaking, it was Jesus. "All your arguments are
just symptoms of the fact that you are right now hardening your will. Recognize your need. Open your heart.
Now. Won't you?"

And that's exactly what I did do. Simply and undramati-
cally, without leaving my seat (I was too proud to do
that), I said yes to Jesus' call. No one in that crowd except
myself knew what I had done. But there was no doubt
in my mind that I had made a breakthrough. In that
fragile moment I put Jesus in the center of my life.

I didn't want Pat to know what I had done. When I
went back to the room he asked me, "How was the meeting?"

"Okay," I said, and went on about my business.

But I wasn't able to fool him. My attitudes changed.
I didn't needle him any more on Sunday mornings before
he left for church. I did my household chores without
digs and groans.

Then one day a month later Pat asked me point blank,

"Dede, something happened to you at Schroon Lake, didn't it?"

I can't say that I gave him a sweet little answer. What I did say, testily, was "Yes, I 'got saved.' I hope you're happy." But my sharpness just went right over Pat's head. He looked at me and smiled.

"Dede," he said, "it's going to make all the difference. You wait and see."

I hoped so. I hoped I'd begin to see some of the much-promised Fruit of the Spirit in my life. How I wanted the peace and gentleness and faith and self-control and joy people talked about, as promised in Galatians 5, instead of the irritability and frustration which—to be honest—were the emotions I really did feel.

When we got back home things weren't much better, on the surface at least. Pat went back to school and so did my sitter, so I quit my job. Pat's pace did not slow down at all. He was overwhelmed by fatigue. He wasn't sleeping right or eating right either, so in addition to a tired man I had a slightly overweight man to contend with. Where was the love, the romance? Where was the tall, interesting young lawyer I married who was such fun? Whenever he wasn't studying, Pat was running from church to church and prayer meeting to prayer meeting, seeking an experience which he called the "Baptism in the Holy Spirit."

GENTLENESS BEANS

I like this savory because I can use it wherever I need a relish.

A sweet and sour relish bean

½ cup sugar
½ cup vinegar
1 onion, thinly sliced
1 cup whole cooked and
  ground soybeans
¼ cup salad oil
1 clove garlic

Bring sugar and vinegar to a boil. Pour over beans with onion and garlic. Add oil last and let stand. Will keep for months in the refrigerator.

2

GENTLENESS

WHAT WAS THIS "BAPTISM," I wondered? It almost seemed as if the experience were seeking Pat, not the other way around. Everywhere he went people started talking to him about that Baptism. He met it in his reading and in casual conversations. He went down to Washington and there he met the editor of *Christian Life* magazine, Bob Walker, who naturally spoke to him about "the Baptism." More and more people at seminary were asking questions on the subject. Chance acquaintances turned out to be people who were just as interested in "the Baptism" as was Pat.

One icy winter's evening, for instance, Pat and I took the subway into Manhattan to attend a banquet. On the ride home, we sat next to a man who had also been at the meeting. Pat introduced us.

"Dede, I don't think you've met Harald Bredesen. Harald's been telling me some more about the Baptism . . ."

And the two of them were off, talking excitedly and loudly above the clatter and roar of the swaying train. Harald was one of God's more unusual people. Just a little heavy, ruddy complexioned, already balding, with what was left of his hair very closely cropped, Harald was dressed entirely in black: black shoes, black sox, black clerical suit and shirt. The only exception was his backwards, round collar which was starchy and white.

"Are you a priest?" I ventured, interrupting the still-animated discussion while we were stopped at a station.

"I'm ordained: a Lutheran," Harald said. "Right now I'm in public relations."

That, certainly, didn't surprise me. Harald was so . . . different. Pat said he got around New York on a *bicycle*. As we all huddled together on the hard seat of the lurching subway car, I felt more than a little embarrassed at the top-of-the-lungs conversation. Pat, however, was delighted and hung on to every word.

We came to our stop and said good-night to Harald. On the platform Pat asked, "Well, Dede, what do you think of him?"

"Harald's an experience. I kept wondering if it was all just an act, but I do believe he's for real."

Harald Bredesen began to play a large role in our lives. He and Pat seemed to spend a great deal of time on the phone talking theology. But it wasn't all talk. One rainy night, just after Pat had left to go to his church in Bayside, there was a knock at our door. I opened it to find Harald standing in the hallway, still dressed all in black, and dripping wet.

"Is it all right if I leave my bicycle locked to a phone pole?" he asked, flicking rainwater from his fingertips. "I mean, in some parts of the city even that's not enough . . ."

Had this man pedalled his way through traffic on a night like this? He began to fish around inside his dripping wet raincoat.

"I was hoping I had the right apartment . . ." His voice trailed off.

"For goodness sake, Harald, come in," I said. "You'll catch your death." Harald stepped through the door and into the foyer, holding a nearly-dry book in his hand. "Is the book for Pat?" I asked.

"Yes. It's about the Holy Ghost," Harald said, handing me the volume. "But I can't stay. Some people are coming over for supper. Gen will be waiting."

So there was a Mrs. Harald Bredesen! I wondered what it would be like, living with this very different man. Harald stayed only long enough to meet Elizabeth and Tim, who stood in the middle of the living room and just stared at this wet man-in-black. Then Harald was off again, but I knew that a new era was beginning. We'd see a lot of Harald Bredesen. And I was right. Not only did Pat continue to spend time talking with Harald on the phone, but Harald soon became a regular member of the Wednesday evening prayer meetings which Pat and his friends from seminary were now holding in our apartment.

Many of the people in this prayer group, of which I was a reluctant but regular member, were to play large roles in our lives over the next few years. Some of these roles were rather mysterious, though they started out in an ordinary manner. For instance, one young woman named Dove Toll often talked about a special dream. She believed that no church could thrive unless it had a strong missionary outreach. Dove wanted to go to Korea to encourage local, Korean Christians to start missionary programs of their own.

What none of us knew was that a complex, divine plan was already in motion. Several years *before* Dove had begun to glimpse her dream, a retired missionary lady

from the Tidewater area of Virginia had invited a Korean
Christian named Mrs. Lea to visit America. While here,
Mrs. Lea and her hostess began to petition God for, of
all things, a Christian television station that might some
day be located in Tidewater. We knew none of this at
the time, and we certainly had no idea that Dove Toll,
sitting in our living room, was involved in an interlocking
fabric which was to prove part of God's provision.

One night several months after these prayer meetings
began, Harald invited the whole group to the Flushing
Full Gospel Church to hear a preacher he admired. It
was a chance to be with Pat for an evening, so we packed
Tim and Elizabeth into the car and drove to Flushing.

As soon as we stepped inside the church I wished I
had stayed home. The building was filled with hand-clap-
ping, radiant worshipers. I was appalled. Pat, though, was
almost on his toes in anticipation.

When the congregation began singing and praying in
a medley of strange sounds, it was my cue to make an
escape. I slipped out to take the children to the nursery
in the church's basement.

There, in the cold, concrete-block nursery, I met a
woman with a daughter about Elizabeth's age.

"You must be Dede Robertson," she said, smiling in
a most friendly fashion. "I recognized you from Harald's
description. After all, there aren't too many women here
with reddish brown hair who are also pregnant."

She introduced herself as Genevieve Bredesen. I was
a bit guarded at first. Anyone married to Harald must
be either a zealot or a mouse. But Gen was neither. She
had her problems living with Harald, I was sure, but she
also seemed to be a very level-headed lady. She referred
to her husband in a light-hearted way. In short I found
her most appealing.

Gen and I talked and talked. About my new baby who was due in a few months, about our husbands' work, about making do on a student's income. Before we knew it, the service upstairs was over. When Harald and Pat came looking for us I found that I was sorry to say good-by to Gen.

On the way home, Pat said, "Dede, you missed a really remarkable experience up in the sanctuary. Harald got a word from God. He is going to start preaching."

"Sounds like Harald all right," I said. "I thought he was in public relations."

"He is, but he's planning to quit when he gets his church."

Three days later out of the blue Harald received a call to become pastor of the historic First Reformed Church in Mount Vernon, just outside New York City. Pat gave me the news excitedly, speaking of it as a confirmation of Harald's word from the Lord. Interesting. Sure enough, Harald would be preaching, and in a prestigious old church, too. I was surprised at the way the series of events warmed my heart.

Pat then redoubled his search for more of the Spirit. Now, instead of just the Wednesday evening prayer meeting in our apartment there were Friday night meetings at various places around New York, not to mention the all-night prayer vigil at Hillside Avenue Presbyterian on Saturday.

Pat seemed to be spending all of his time with his fellow seekers from school. Dark-haired, soft-spoken, Dick White and fiery, zealous Dick Simmons, so it seemed to me, were spending almost every waking hour with Pat in prayer. Often I prayed that the Lord would baptize them quickly, before they all zoomed up to heaven. I wondered how Gen could have tolerated all this activity. Then a terrible thought pierced my heart: if Pat was active now, what would he be like once he received the much-vaunted energy of the Baptism!

During one of our hausfrau get-togethers, I asked Gen how she was able to cope with Harald's life in the Holy Spirit. Her reply hit me hard.

"Well, Dede," Gen said, "I've received the Baptism, too."

I don't know why it had never occurred to me that the special, warm and supportive quality I saw in Gen might also be a manifestation of the Holy Spirit.

As the months passed I began to bridle at the life most young mothers are asked to lead. I was pretty well confined to the apartment. I would go to the playground at the front of our building as often as I could, just to be around other mothers; otherwise I would have been immersing myself totally in the children's Lilliputian world. It made me feel guilty that I wanted to be away from the children. I knew I should be treasuring these precious moments with them. And the trouble was that the moments *were* precious. Elizabeth would come toddling up to me swathed in my silk scarves. Then her older brother would dash into the room with his brilliant red hair and blue eyes alive.

"Look, Mom; I'm Roy Rogers," he'd cry over his shoulder, and I would strifle a laugh at the thought of this little guy rounding up bad varmints. *Why isn't Pat here to see this?* I'd wonder to myself, almost angry at Pat and students in general who were always so busy. Why did Pat put us through so much so fast when a young family's life is hectic anyway?

On the other hand Pat's strengths were clear to me, too. I don't think I have ever known a more honest man. In dealing with the churches where he worked as a student, Pat paid close attention to the details of honesty.

He was supposed to put in a certain number of hours for his paycheck; whenever there was a question as to whether an hour belonged to the church or to Pat, the church got the benefit. In school, whenever he was writing a paper, he was careful to footnote ideas that were not his own. He was a man of principle even when it cost him. For example, he just did not believe in raffles. One day I entered a raffle held by the residents of our apartment building to pay for equipment on the playground. I won. But Pat made me take back my loot. The neighbors, I must say, thought we were crazy.

There was also a mysterious power about Pat. He was no normal convert. I agreed with the people who were forever telling me, "That Pat of yours, the Lord's really got a big job for him!" What they did not add was that there was a price tag to that "big job." We could never be just plain, normal people.

Then there was the intrusion upon our family privacy, especially via the telephone. It was usually one of Pat's friends from seminary, like Dick White or Dick Simmons or Alice Blair or Dove Toll or Gene Peterson, excited about some spiritual happening.

The Baptism in the Holy Spirit was the usual topic. Pat was convinced that this experience was meant for all who followed Christ. He kept talking about the power of the Spirit and how much he wanted to receive the "gift of tongues."

"Look, Pat," I objected, "this Baptism has been around for 2,000 years. Couldn't you stay home a few nights? Maybe the experience will come *to* you."

Pat just stared at me. Anything worthwhile was to be sought with vigor.

At this juncture, a new minister was hired at the church where Pat was a student assistant. By custom, any new pastor had the privilege of choosing his own assistant, so changes would be coming soon. Harald took the opportunity to hire Pat as his assistant.

It was a happy time, that spring of 1958, because on June 4 my one-month-overdue baby arrived. We named him Gordon. He was a delightful addition to our family. I was pleased, too, with Pat's new job because I would be seeing more of Gen. I had prayed for a friend who would help me understand my life with Pat; Gen was the answer to that prayer. Gen was a real help to me. She never told me I was right when she thought otherwise. We faced many of the same problems. We both had young children and we both had husbands who had very, very demanding work to do. Gen also taught me the rudiments of trusting God in a marriage. Harald might show up at the parsonage with 15 people in tow, ". . . just for a snack, please, Gen?" It was pure chaos at times in the old parsonage where the Bredesens lived in the midst of dust and bricks while the building was being repaired. Gen didn't always handle the tension too well. But she did hold on to one central idea, and it made all the difference to me in my own relationship with Pat.

"God made Harald," she said to me one day when I was visiting her. "And then He gave Harald to me. It's my job now to trust what He has done."

Shortly after Pat joined Harald he entered a new level in his search for the Baptism. For the first time, he seemed to be striving instead of seeking. One morning he came careening through the kitchen not even noticing the breakfast I'd prepared.

"I'm late for my meeting with Harald!" he exclaimed, grabbing a muffin off the table as he ran past.

"Why don't you just have all of your meals at the church from now on?" I snapped. "I'm not wasting any more time cooking for you!"

He was halfway through the door when he did a classic double-take, not sure he had heard right.

"That's right," I continued. "You're becoming more and more impossible to live with. If God is eager to give you what you need, then you've simply got to stop chasing Him."

"I'm not 'chasing' Him, Dede. I'm seeking to claim His promises."

"Seeking, claiming, chasing . . . what difference does it make? If the Lord wants you to have something, He can give it to you right here at home."

By this time my tears were starting to show and Pat realized he had to come back and sit down, even if he did miss his date with Harald.

"Okay, Dede, I'm sorry. Please forgive me. Really, I love you. Very much indeed. But I just *know* there's power out there for me to do the work I think God is calling me to."

"Do you think God doesn't know that, Pat? Do you think He is trying to *tease* you with His Spirit so that your family is demolished?"

Pat was quiet for a long while. Then he said with a great deal of resignation, "Maybe you're right, Dede. Maybe I'm running after the Baptism too hard."

Pat ate another muffin that morning. I didn't say anything more. I was too busy rejoicing.

One afternoon about a week later, I put Gordon in the carriage and started out to the grocery with Tim and Elizabeth walking beside me. Our usually pleasant Timmy was whiny and crabby. I put my hand to his forehead. He was feverish.

I forgot my trip and quickly returned home. I made a bed for Tim on the living room sofa, plumped up a pillow and put him down. As the afternoon progressed, Timmy's temperature began to rise. This was typical for a sick child, but toward evening Tim seemed to be getting more and more flushed.

I called the pediatrician. His office was closed but the answering service said they'd try to locate him. More time passed and I was beginning to grow concerned. Pat came home. I told him the news. Pat knelt at the couch.

"Timmy, Timmy can you hear me? It's Dad."

Tim just groaned. His face was flaming red against the stark white pillow case.

"Did you call the doctor, Dede?"

"Yes, but he hasn't answered yet. Pat, you'd better start rubbing him down with alcohol while I try again." As I dialed, Pat disappeared into the bathroom and reappeared with the bottle of rubbing alcohol. His hands were fumbling with the cap. He knelt down again at the side of the couch. In his anxiety he spilled the liquid as he poured it onto the face cloth.

The doctor's answering service number rang endlessly. Suddenly, Pat called for me.

"Dede, you'd better come here!" I dropped the receiver and rushed over. As Pat sponged Timmy's feverish body the boy was becoming stiff and rigid.

"It's a muscle spasm, Pat. He's on the verge of a convulsion!"

"What'll we do?"

"I don't know what to do. The alcohol isn't helping."

Pat got down on his knees and looked up and said, "Oh, Heavenly Father, please, please do something."

I knelt down next to him and prayed, too, not at all self-consciously.

"Please, Lord," Pat prayed, "I know I've been away a lot, but You love Timmy. Please, Lord, please help him." Pat's face was tight and contorted. He was biting his lip

and his eyes were tightly closed. "Timmy is Your child.
We lift him up to You."

"Thank You, Father. Thank You, Lord," I said.

We were letting go of Timmy. Instead of trying to heal
him with our own strength, we were letting God take
over and work His will.

Within minutes, Timmy began to perspire.

A few minutes more and his color returned. He felt
cooler. I took his temperature and it was practically normal.

Timmy opened his eyes, looked at us, and then pushed
himself onto his elbow. He smiled.

"Oh, thank You, Jesus. Thank You, Lord!" Pat repeated
over and over. I watched in silence as Pat continued to
praise God for Timmy's healing.

Then it happened!

Pat's praises turned into a language I just couldn't understand. For a long time I watched in silence as Pat
knelt, praying before our little boy who was resting quietly. Finally Pat saw me.

"When did you receive the Baptism, Pat?" I whispered.

"It just happened, Honey. Right now, as we were thank-
ing God."

"Oh, Pat, I'm so happy for you! And I'm so glad the
Lord gave you His Baptism when we were together. See,
it happened right in your own living room." We were
laughing and crying at the same time.

Pat, of course, had to tell Harald. As he dialed I sat
holding Tim's hand, thinking about the message that had
been coming to me. There was a special quietness and
assurance that came to people when they gave up struggling and turned things over to God, trusting in His goodness. They didn't have to try to control things.

Pat was shouting the good news to Harald. After a while
he handed the phone to me. Gen was on the line.

"Dede," Gen asked, "what do you want more than anything else right now?"

What an interesting question. Gen must have sensed the power that was surging into our little apartment and wanted to take advantage of it. I knew the answer right away. It had to do with my recent harshness with Pat. "I've been so unsympathetic," I said.

"Let's give this a name, Dede," Gen said. "Instead of taking something away, let's ask the Lord to *give* you something. What would you like to ask for?"

"Gentleness," was my quick reply.

I heard a merry laugh on the other end of the line. Gen understood all too well. We prayed together over the phone and said good-by.

That night I tried to talk with Pat about what was happening. Pat answered drowsily. The poor guy! Even after an exhilarating experience like today's he was so exhausted he fell asleep almost before he was in bed.

God *is* good, I said as I lay there in the dark, listening to the healthy breathing of our little boy. Where would He lead me next? What spiritual fruit might He provide now? I tried to remember all nine of the Fruit of the Spirit, but couldn't. Perhaps it was just as well. For the next lesson He taught me was in the area of *patience*, and to a reddish haired girl with a little Irish blood in her veins, patience doesn't come easily.

PATIENCE BEANS

This was the first soybean dish we tried.

½ cup chopped onion
¼ lb. diced salt pork or ham
¾ cup brown sugar or molasses
½ cup catsup

1 t dried mustard
2 t salt
1 T Worcestershire sauce
1 t curry powder
3 cups soybeans (soaked overnight and drained)

Mix all ingredients, place in oven-proof casserole. Decorate top with more salt pork or ham. Bake covered in a *slow* oven 250° for 6 to 8 hours. If beans become dry, add water in small amounts. Uncover for last hour of baking. Serves eight.

3

PATIENCE

UP UNTIL THE WINTER of 1958 I had always thought that Pat was tired because he wasn't getting enough sleep. But lately I'd begun to realize that we were facing a deeper problem. Pat just wasn't getting the right food into his system. If his work allowed him to be at home regularly, I could monitor his eating habits. But he wasn't at home, and whenever I asked him what he had eaten that day the answer was the same. A hot dog. A quick hamburger. A cup of coffee. A Danish. No wonder he was losing vitality.

So I had Pat's depleted energy very much in mind on that Sunday afternoon in mid-March 1959 when I was introduced all over again to the soybean—not in a college textbook this time, but in a delicious casserole.

Once a month Harald Bredesen's church in Mount Vernon held a covered dish supper in the social hall. On this blustery, late afternoon Pat and I piled the kids into the old blue DeSoto my mother and father had given us three years earlier when they moved to the Middle

43

East, and headed through city traffic for nearby Mount Vernon.

The First Reformed Church was perched on the side of a hill in the heart of Mount Vernon. Built in the late 1800s, the old church had walls that were black with age. The social hall where we held our suppers was a bit dreary in spite of the bank of windows which was supposed to bring in sunshine. The windows were so dirty with city grime that not much light made its way to the sooty walls. Yet somehow, with flower arrangements or gay crepe paper tablecloths, Gen and the ladies in the church turned this dull room into a cheerful, colorful place.

As usual when we trudged up the rickety stairs to the social hall we made a dramatic entrance. Four-year-old Tim was the family's big boy who always raced up the stairs ahead of everyone. Elizabeth, with a fierce competitive spirit at two and one-half, thumped after him shouting, "I can so beat you to the top." I carried a molded salad in one arm and on the other I carried Gordon, who was a very content, happily gurgling nine-month-old. The thumping and banging and racing on that staircase made it seem as if a tribe of wild men were attacking the social hall.

"Okay kids, settle down and stop when you get to the top of the stairs," shouted Pat.

Timmy and Elizabeth halted obediently and waited for us. As we climbed the last few steps we could see the bright florescent-lighted kitchen on the right. Exciting smells wafted toward us as we stepped into the large church hall with its big wall of windows.

The children shrieked with delight when they saw the long tables set with colorful paper cloths and matching paper cups and napkins. Each table had a vase containing flowers from the bouquet used in church that morning.

Even gray walls looked golden as the setting sun cast its long slanting rays into the room.

Gen was expecting her second child. Dressed in a flower-print maternity dress and followed by Harald and little Dagni, Gen met us at the top of the stairs to help with the children's coats.

At first it seemed like any ordinary buffet. I walked over to the serving table to set down my molded salad, and looked around me. What an array of food! Orange carrots, green olives and red radishes dotted the tables. A dish of Swedish meatballs was placed next to a pan of crispy, batter-fried chicken. You could almost hear how crunchy that chicken was going to be.

And then one of the members of a Bible study group at Harald's church came to the table carrying a steaming casserole.

"Is that your usual, Dora?" Gen asked, making room and introducing me to her friend. Dora was a dark-haired, very proper southern lady. She set the "usual" down and lifted the cover to check it. "Oh, that looks better than ever," Gen said after a quick peek. I could smell the "usual" but couldn't see it.

Harald said the blessing and we all formed a line at the serving table. Dora was in front of me and Pat just behind me. I was glad to see him filling his plate with salads and protein instead of carbohydrates.

Then we came to Dora's casserole.

I leaned forward and looked more closely. It certainly smelled good, but the ingredients were unfamiliar to me. Its main ingredient had a slight resemblance to black-eyed peas, but without the color or shape of any peas with which I was familiar. They were lighter in color, almost round. There were pieces of diced ham mixed into the casserole, and the whole dish was sprinkled with parsley.

"What's this, Dede?" Pat asked.

"I don't know, Honey. Ham and peas?"

"Not really," said Dora, looking backwards over her shoulder. "It's a mixture of Smithfield ham and soybeans."

"Soybeans!" Pat was incredulous. "You mean the stuff they use for feeding cows?"

Dora laughed. "Actually," she said, "soybeans are one of God's best sources of protein."

As soon as she said that, my mind did a flashback to my days at Yale. I remembered that soybeans were called "nutritional gold," because they were a nearly perfect, nonmeat protein. If I were looking for a high quality energy food that we could afford, was this my answer?

I watched carefully as Pat took the large serving spoon and placed a *tiny* bit of Dora's "usual" on his plate. He put an even smaller amount on his fork and gingerly tasted it. Dora and I watched him.

Then his eyes opened wide. He took a larger forkful and said, "Dora, they're good! Dede, try them. They're delicious."

I put a spoonful on my plate and tasted them. They had the texture of baked beans with an added, mysterious, nutlike taste. And with the smoked ham added, there was a truly interesting combination of flavors. Toward the end of the evening Dora handed Pat a paperback copy of one of Adelle Davis' books on nutrition.

"You might be interested in this," Dora said. Pat took the book from her and leafed through it. "You can keep it," Dora said. "It's not just about soybeans; it's a total concept of nutrition."

"Thank you." Pat looked at the book. He seemed very interested. Then he handed it to me. "Dede's the nutrition expert, though."

When I started looking through that book, there in the social hall of Harald's church, a strange thing happened. I was more interested than I could account for, as if I were being challenged. Not just by soybeans, but by what Dora called "a total concept of nutrition."

The rest of the evening was frustrating to me. I was eager to get home and dig out my college textbooks on nutrition. At last we bundled up our drooping kids, kissed Gen and Harald good-by, then headed into the blustery March night.

Back home we put the children straight to bed— Timmy and Elizabeth in one bedroom, Gordon in a crib in our room. We *were* getting crowded!

Pat went to bed but I didn't. Tonight the sofa was mine. I searched the bookcase next to the sofa until I found the volumes I wanted. There was an unusual calm about the room. Perhaps it was the soft play of lights and the low bubbling sounds that came from the fish tank on top of the bookcase. Or perhaps it was the serene shades of blue in the chairs that I had just slipcovered, or the order that flowed out of our family rule that the children's playthings had to be picked up at the end of the day. I didn't know, but the Lord seemed to have put me into a very receptive, unhurried mood, as if He wanted my full attention.

So I stretched out, said a quiet "thank You" for nudging me to look into this new provision, then opened my books. I read again what I had learned in school, that the history of the soybean is clouded with mystery. Some sources claim the bean was cultivated in the Mediterranean Valley as early as 5000 B.C., others that it dates back to the days of a Chinese emperor, Shen-Nung, who lived around 2830 B.C. Odd that soybeans weren't introduced to America until the nineteenth century.

This was all interesting, but it wasn't what I needed to know right now. Ah, yes, there it was: the reason why the soy is called nutritional gold.

The soybean is perhaps the world's most important legume because of its unusually high nutritive value. Besides its unusual power to satisfy hunger, it provides calcium, iron, phosphorus, potassium. It also provides vitamins A, B-complex and C. The soybean really is a miracle food. It has one and a half times as much protein for its weight as cheese, peas or navy beans, twice as much protein, ounce for ounce, as meat or fish, three times as much as eggs or whole wheat flour, and eleven times as much as milk! And—very important for our waistlines—soybeans have a much lower carbohydrate content than other shell beans.

But it is for still another reason that soys are such a provision from God. Protein is constructed of a series of building blocks known as amino acids. Soybeans are a nearly perfect source of the essential amino acids which our bodies need. They contain all but two, and as for the two—methionine and tryptophas—they can easily be supplied by adding different combinations of food. Soybeans with brown rice and bulger wheat, for example, make for a complete amino acid content. Other dishes that complement the soybean, the books in my lap told me, are corn and milk, or peanuts and sesame.

I put my books down for a minute. I knew that if I could change Pat's diet to high-energy food, he would feel better. Like most wives, probably, I was already doing all I could to give my family a balanced diet. But our problem was *protein*, which was another way of saying that our problem was money. We just couldn't often afford the traditional high-protein foods I knew were vital to good health. But perhaps this very day I was being given the answer.

I finally turned off the light and went to bed thinking about the legume that my textbook called "the meat that grows on vines."

The next morning I felt on top of the world. Pat came into the kitchen, kissed me on the cheek, and sat down to eat.

"On your way home, Pat, would you please pick up a little smoked ham? I'll get some soybeans, and tonight we're going to have a casserole like Dora's."

"Sounds great, Dede. I'll be home early."

"For once, Pat?"

As usual, he didn't rise to my bait. He got up, reached for his coat with one hand, finished his coffee with the other, and left in such a hurry that I felt we were in a movie where the reel is set permanently on fast-forward.

After the breakfast dishes were cleared away, the children and I went to the health-food store not far from our building. I walked down the aisle slowly until I found a package wrapped in cellophane with a handwritten label, "Soybeans." I paid the long-haired girl and left the store clutching my treasure in a brown paper bag.

I couldn't wait to try out this dish. Later that morning, while the children were napping, I had a chance to look at the soybeans. I picked up the crinkly-sounding package and looked for instructions on the label. There were none. The packer had apparently decided that any legume which has been around for 5000 years doesn't need instructions. In that case, it couldn't be too difficult . . .

So I opened the package and took my chances. I ran the tan-gold beans through my fingers and started to sort them, removing the cracked and shriveled ones, just as I would do with kidney beans or lentils. Then I washed them thoroughly, took out a big pot, filled it with water, put in some salt and dumped in the beans.

After the first hour of slow cooking, I realized that soybeans require patience. They looked exactly the same as when I put them in the water, except that some foam had formed on the top. I put one of the beans in my mouth. It didn't show the first sign of tenderness.

Tim woke up, came into the kitchen and stopped just inside the door. He sniffed the air, wrinkled his nose and said, "What smells so awful, Mom?"

Casually, I replied, "Oh, a new dish, Honey."

Tim left to play with Elizabeth. He was right, the soybeans *didn't* smell too interesting. So I found an onion and peeled it and stuck in a lot of cloves for added flavor. I threw the onion into my brew along with a carrot and a stalk of celery. I peered into the pot again. They were all boiling merrily. Well, we'd see.

The children and I played inside until midafternoon, while my soybeans cooked and cooked and cooked. I stirred them regularly, adding water every now and then, but each time I tested one it didn't seem to be very tender. When the children had finished their word games, they decided that they wanted to go outside. So I turned the gas down to a bare simmer, covered the pot with a tight-fitting lid, and we went out.

Funny how often the Lord was using the playground as a time to speak to me. As I sat in the chill sun, I began to think about what the Lord was doing with Pat and me. As we opened ourselves up, He was slowly, patiently manifesting the Fruit of the Spirit in our lives.

"And now," I said to Him as I lifted my face to the sun, "are You saying something about *patience?* I'm not at all patient with Pat. I'm impatient with myself too." Then I had to laugh. "I'm even impatient with soybeans, Lord! I get annoyed when they aren't tender and tasty right away. Those little beans are just me all over—hard kernels that require a lot of slow preparations before they're worth much."

The day was nippy, and there was just enough breeze to make us go back indoors. I peeked into the pot. A lot of the water had been absorbed so I tried one of the beans. It was still very tough! "Well," I said, adding more water and turning up the gas, "they'll be fine by the time I'm ready to add the ham."

True to his word, Pat arrived home by five that evening with a shank of smoked ham. "Sure was expensive," he said, as he handed it to me.

It didn't matter that we could afford only a little ham. Soybeans, Dora had told me, pick up the flavor of other ingredients. Even a small amount of meat, diced and stirred in, should give its flavor to the entire casserole.

I tossed part of the ham into the soybeans and let them simmer another twenty minutes while I finished cooking more carrots. I put a leafy green salad on the table, got out a large serving dish, ladled in my prize meal, garnished it with fresh parsley, and placed the dish beside the salad. I clapped my hands twice and called, "Dinner is served, everyone."

We sat down and Pat said the blessing. Then he took the large spoon, served all of us and, smacking his lips, heaped soybeans and ham onto his own plate.

Tim and Elizabeth looked at their plates suspiciously. They watched Pat and waited to take their cue from him. No one was talking. Gordon, unaccustomed to such silence, jiggled in his highchair and gave a few attention-demanding squeals.

"Come on, kids, eat. You'll love this," said Pat.

He took a large forkful. But Tim and Elizabeth reminded me of Pat the first time he tasted the dish. Each took about two soybeans onto his fork. And as they began to eat I watched their expressions.

Pat wrinkled up his nose and swallowed hard.

Elizabeth and Tim made faces and in unison said, "Yuck."

I tasted mine. "They *are* a bit crunchy," I had to admit.

I tried another bit. "Every now and then in the kitchen I tested them, Pat, and somehow they didn't seem quite this tough."

"We'll be lucky if our teeth survive," whispered Pat.

"Eat the ham part, children," I said and gave them lots of carrots and salad.

Pat and I tried our best to eat what we could of the casserole, but it was no use. Those beans were just too tough! "Maybe you'd better give Dora a call," Pat said.

So that was the end of our feast. The chunks of ham disappeared and so did the salad, the carrots and even the onion. But the helpings of soybeans on each plate remained untouched.

Left to myself I probably would have dropped the idea of conquering these little beans in spite of their reputed miracle food value. But Pat surprised me by urging me to try again.

"These beans may be God's way of keeping us well, Dede," Pat reminded me. "Don't give up. If I bring some more home, will you call Dora to see what you're doing wrong?"

With a flick of returning enthusiasm I said I was game, and sure enough, the very next night Pat came home with a huge brown paper bag. "Here you are, Sweetheart—nutritional gold." Pat put the bag on the kitchen table and opened it while the children watched skeptically. I ran some through my fingers. They did appear to be plumper than the ones from the health foods store, but even so I waited until the next Sunday to tell Dora about my disaster.

"Your instincts were right," Dora said, laughing. "You always discard any shriveled or discolored beans. Then measure out the amount you want. A cup of dry beans gives about two and a half cups of cooked soybeans."

"And then . . . ? What's the secret?"

Dora chuckled. "You're right. There is a secret. Soaking. Overnight."

"Of course."

"The water," Dora explained, "also carries off a lot of the carbohydrates that make for difficult digestion and flatulence."* After she filled me in on a few more hints, such as adding olive oil to the water to keep down foaming, I was ready to try again.

That evening I started over. As I flipped through the cookbook that Dora had given us, I saw that there was a faster method of preparing soybeans, by freezing them after they had soaked for two hours and before they are cooked. I learned, too, that the beans can be made into a meal by running the soaked and cooked beans through a blender or by grinding them. One day soon, I said to myself, I wanted to try that.

But right now I was determined to make Dora's casserole properly. Since it was already late, I chose the faster method. I soaked the beans for two hours and then froze them overnight in ice cube trays in the freezing compartment of our refrigerator.

Next morning I dropped the frozen soybeans into hot water to thaw them and added an onion, garlic, salt and peppercorns. When Tim came into the kitchen a little later he sniffed and made no comment.

"They'll taste better this time, Timmy. I promise."

Then I baked the soybeans, which were now thawed and boiling, and the hambone from our earlier disaster, for about six hours, drained the water, added some mo-

---

* I was worried about flatulence too. But later I found there were three secrets: first, allow *plenty* of time for soaking, preferably overnight; second, add meat tenderizer to the water during soaking; and third, don't be afraid to cook the beans long enough to become really tender; soybeans will hardly ever become mushy.

lasses and ketchup, and the remainder of our ham. Now and then the kids came around sniffing. Pat did, too, when he came home. "Well, it *smells* good," he said.

Again we sat down, Pat said grace and then served our plates. The children waited, watching Pat. Then they timidly tested their own food.

It would be an exaggeration to say that they were over-joyed, but on the other hand they did smile a bit too, and they cleaned up their plates while Pat encouraged them with comments about the meal. They were comments which, I sensed, were more than just Pat-being-kind.

SELF-CONTROL CHILI

Tim eats this dish mainly because he doesn't know it's made with soybeans.

2 T suet, fat or oil
3 cups cooked soybeans, ground
1 large chopped onion
1 clove garlic, minced

1 t oregano
1 t cumin seed
6 t (or more) chili powder
2 medium cans tomatoes

3 cups cooked soybeans, whole
or
3 cups cooked chili beans
or
1½ cups each

In a large skillet, combine fat, ground soybeans, onion, garlic and brown lightly. Transfer to large pot. Add oregano, cumin seed, chili powder, tomatoes, whole portion of soybeans. Cover with water and bring to boil, lower heat and simmer at least one hour.

Ground beef and pork may be substituted for equal amount of the ground soybeans. Serves four.

SELF-CONTROL

AND SO IT WAS that we began an experiment in good nutrition.

Soybeans of course weren't some sort of magic cure-all. If we had had lots of money we wouldn't need them at all. I had tried to get Pat to join the children and me in the "Basic Four": fruit and vegetables; milk and dairy products; cereal; meat, fish, eggs or other high-protein foods. The trouble came with the high protein part of this ideal, balanced diet. Whenever possible we ate meat, but except for beef liver which the children hated, we really couldn't afford high-protein foods very often. And in addition, I had Pat's personality to contend with. Far too often I would prepare a well-balanced breakfast only to have him rush out because he was late for an appointment. I knew what would happen later. He would run out of energy and grab a quick cup of coffee. He himself spoke of it as his "coffee and Danish way of life."

Even so, both Pat and I were determined to switch from a high carbohydrate to a high protein diet. As we began to make the change I heard Pat telling his friends

57

that the new eating pattern made a considerable difference. Poor Pat. He used to ask the Lord to deliver him from sloth. He thought he was being lazy, when in fact he just wasn't giving his body the right fuel.

Pat's seminary days were coming to an end in that spring of 1959. He would be graduating in June, three months away.

As the day drew closer, I found myself once again playfully imagining what it would be like when Pat had his new degree. Perhaps he'd be called to a fine church in a fine neighborhood where we'd have excellent schools and stimulating companions. The fantasy reminded me of my Yale days when I dreamed about the glamorous life of leisure Pat and I would have together, a world of candlelight and servants.

Well, that dream certainly had not come true. I laughed when I realized that we had eaten another soybean casserole the night before, a dish which I called "Self-Control Chili." We'd eaten it at the kitchen table in our tiny apartment in Queens, surrounded by our three children who had me as their "nanny."

Never mind, my imaginary tomorrow was still fun. Sometimes when Pat was late getting home from Mount Vernon I would sit in our living room in Queens and try to visualize how my furniture would look in the Hollywood-style manse. The maple chairs were much too casual, of course. They would be better suited to the den. Everything would have its own place, and we could get rid of the lineup at the foyer door, which would soon be including a tricycle for Elizabeth and a riding toy for Gordon, gifts from their grandparents.

Pat really enjoyed working with Harald Bredesen, and we were both sorry when Harald told us that the job was coming to an end. Harald's parish simply could not support an associate. So Pat had to start looking for his own church sooner than we had expected. He went "candidating," as the students nicknamed the process of job hunting. Pat reported that most of the leads supplied by the seminary were to fine old churches in good locations with comfortable manses. We prayed together about each possibility, although we also agreed that Pat himself had to make the final decision.

Then one Sunday Pat came home from a visit to an old Presbyterian church in the Bedford-Stuyvesant section of Brooklyn. Our friends, Dick and Barbara Simmons, who had already graduated, had accepted a position there the previous fall. The area was a ghetto. I hadn't wanted Pat even to visit Bedford-Stuyvesant because of its reputation for violence. Every day, it seemed, the papers carried a story of some new horror. Gang wars, murder, rape, muggings, all were normal occurrences on the streets of this once-elegant section of New York.

But Pat went to Bedford-Stuyvesant in spite of my wifely caution. I knew we were headed for trouble when he came in all smiles that afternoon. He settled himself on the sofa and in a much too friendly way patted the cushion next to him.

"Come, sit down for a minute, Dede."

I didn't bite. I pulled up the blue chair and sat down in front of him.

"What is it, Pat? You found Brooklyn a challenge, didn't you?"

"Yes, and there's a big roomy manse," Pat rushed on as he quickly loosened his tie.

"And are you sitting there telling me that the Robertsons are going to join the Simmons in a New York ghetto?" As soon as the words were out of my mouth I realized the sharpness behind them. *Oh, Dede,* I said to myself, *when will you ever learn to control yourself!*

Pat looked at me for a long time without answering.

We had agreed together again that deciding where he should minister was basically Pat's choice, but I hoped he wouldn't seriously consider a violent part of the world. Bedford-Stuyvesant might be all right for people who had a special call, like the Simmons. Dick and Barbara were unusual people. They had a child, Paul, six months older than Gordon, who was born with motor-neurological retardation but was kept at home in spite of advice that he be institutionalized. This took courage. Fortunately, since most of the little boy's care would fall on Barbara, she was a calm and easy-going person.

Now Paul was nearly two and Barbara was just about to give birth again, in June. She had such a selfless nature that all who met her were drawn by it. Dick was not afraid to tackle anything. As a couple, they would be a real gift to Bedford-Stuyvesant.

So why was I uneasy? What did the Simmons' decision have to do with us? As soon as I asked the question I knew the answer: I was remembering something Dick Simmons had said the previous November just after he received the call to this church in the slums. Dick told us that he had not been surprised at the call. The Lord had already told him in prayer that he was going to be sent to a place where he had no desire to go!

That was what terrified me.

"O Lord," I said under my breath, "that's what You're saying to me, too, isn't it? You're going to send us where we have no desire to go . . . to the slums."

Sure enough, the subject of Bedford-Stuyvesant kept coming up. The parishioners at his church, Dick told us on the phone, were so delighted to have a minister who actually wanted to live in the long-abandoned manse that they volunteered to renovate the building.

One morning in June 1959, just before graduation, Bar-

bara called and asked me to come over to Brooklyn to
see her brand new baby, Mary Elizabeth. Pat thought
it was all right.

"You can drive the car there easily," Pat said. "Take
Gordon with you. I'll watch Tim and Elizabeth."

If Dick and Barbara could *live* in the slums I could
at least visit there. I didn't really feel I had any choice
but to dress Gordon in his new red suit and white shirt
and go. Pat carried the stroller out to the old DeSoto
for me. And, armed with careful directions, I drove off.

As I made my way toward Bedford-Stuyvesant, the
neighborhoods began to deteriorate. Litter blew across
the streets. Overturned cans of garbage were everywhere. Old people hovered in doorways. On one corner
a group of teenagers were drinking wine in a burned-
out automobile.

Then I came to the intersection of Classon and Monroe
where the church stood. The building had been the grand
old lady of this once-fine neighborhood. The large, stone
structure which probably held more than a thousand people may have been white at some time in the past, but
its soot-streaked exterior told the story of years of neglect.
It had beautiful, stained-glass windows which, I was surprised to notice, had not been broken.

Down the street from the church was the four-story
brownstone manse where Dick and Barbara lived. *Why
am I looking at all this so closely?* I asked myself.

A parking place opened up in front of the brownstone
and I backed in. Almost immediately, the heavy front
door opened and Dick and Barbara both came out. Barbara, cradling the new baby in her arms, and Dick, holding Paul, came down the brownish, stone steps to greet
Gordon and me. We all stood on the sidewalk that spring
morning and while neighborhood children gawked un-
selfconsciously, Barbara held tiny, healthy Mary Eliza-

beth down for Gordon to see. I put the stroller down for a minute and I guess Dick thought I was going to leave it outside.

"I'll take that for you," he said. "We can't leave it out here." He didn't have to explain why.

We entered the manse. The first things that caught my attention were the number of *people* everywhere, and the fact that there was a lot of laughter. Dick and Barbara made no attempt to introduce their friends individually beyond explaining that they were "residents" and "helpers."

When my eyes adjusted to the dark entrance hall I could make out a wide staircase which led to upper floors. To the left were two once-grand rooms: a parlor, and a dining room with high ceilings and tall windows. In the parlor there was a blue slipcovered sofa and two chairs, and in the dining room there was an old-fashioned, almost black, mahogany set that seemed to absorb most of the already dim light. One touch I did admire in each room were the large fireplaces framed by ornately carved woodwork.

"If you want the complete tour," Barbara said, "we'll start with the kitchen. It's down in the basement." Again I wondered why I *felt* as if I were being shown a house in which I would one day live.

I held Gordon close, for some reason, as we went down gloomy back stairs to the bottom floor of the old brownstone. When we stepped into the very large kitchen, I was appalled at the primitive conditions. Through two windows directly in front of me I could see a grassless, fenced-in back yard. Under the windows stood a funny looking white poreclain sink on spindly legs, with an extension at one end to use as a drainboard.

Between this sink and the back door were a modern washer and a dryer, looking totally out of place, and a gas stove which was being used. I recognized the smell: soybeans. The feature that dominated the room, however, was a large wooden door to which someone had attached a set of legs so that it could be used as a dining table. The door-table was covered with a patterned oilcloth and was surrounded by an assortment of mismatched chairs.

While Dick stayed downstairs, Barbara and I took our three children up to the parlor. Barbara, not surprisingly, seemed tired. Holding two-weeks-old Mary Elizabeth in one arm, she brushed off a chair, sending a cloud of dust into the air. All this grime and confusion! People everywhere. The dust, a brand new baby—how could Barbara stand it! I put Gordon down for only a moment and was immediately sorry. Right away he was covered with soot, his suit and shirt almost instantly grimy with black streaks. Barbara laughed at my astonishment.

"We're cleaner than we used to be, Dede," she said shrugging her shoulders. "You wouldn't believe what this place looked like when we first got here."

"I think I would, Barbara." I couldn't go on; I was on the verge of tears. I could understand the motivation that drew people into helpful, supportive work. I had a similar streak inside me, too—that was what led me to go into nursing, after all. But there was something so depressing about Bedford-Stuyvesant! "It may be all right for you, Barbara," I lashed out in defiance. "But I could *never* live here!"

All the way home I told myself how glad I was we'd been saved from Bedford-Stuyvesant. The place unnerved me, and that made me feel guilty because it was so obvious that Dick and Barbara—and Pat too—were willing to live anywhere God sent them. How did they manage this attitude?

Finally, I reached our own neighborhood and parked

the car. I put Gordon in his stroller and, hoping I wouldn't meet anyone who would recognize this dirty child, I trekked the short, remaining distance to our home. Tim's tricycle was gone which meant that Pat wasn't in yet. The very minute I got past the lineup, I went into the bathroom where I soaked Gordon until his skin wrinkled like a prune.

When Pat came in with the other children half an hour later, I burst out with my feelings. "I will never, ever go back to Bedford-Stuyvesant, Pat. It's dangerous. It's grimy. I would have sterilized Gordon if I could have."

A shadow passed over Pat's face. It lasted for just a moment, but I saw it.

"Sit down a minute, Honey. It couldn't have been all that bad."

"Well, Pat, it was."

"Dick said there are some real possibilities there," Pat went on, as if he hadn't heard me. My heart began to pound. What was Pat doing, defending that slum in this way?

"And he's going to let seminary students share the house," Pat went on, telling me what I already knew. "Dick White, maybe. Alice Blair. The manse will be sort of a communal parsonage. There's a big need in Bedford-Stuyvesant, Dede. In fact, if Jesus were being born today, I'll bet He'd be born in a place like Bedford-Stuyvesant."

Pat's voice droned on. But I was no longer listening. What was he trying to do? I just wouldn't . . . I tried to master my emotions. It was a bootstrap effort, to be sure, but I just didn't know any other way to self-control.

I needed to change the subject and as quickly as possible. "Tell me, Pat, how was your day?"

"Well I heard about a church in the east 60s, near the Barbizon Hotel."

The east 60s! That was good news. Manhattan's east

60s was an area of tree-lined streets and well-kept town-houses and uniformed maids pushing prams.

The next day Pat went to visit that church. They liked him, and sure enough he was offered a position. We prayed about it, but did not get a go-ahead. I was disappointed, not only because the church was in a safe neighborhood, but also because we needed a steady income. Most of the graduating students at the seminary had already taken positions. It didn't help when Mother wrote from Lebanon wondering when Pat was going to start holding down a job.

Then, shortly after Pat's graduation, came a totally unexpected phone call, one that was to set the course of our lives for the next month.

Pat was home a lot these days since he was "candidating" in the New York area. Early one afternoon he and the children were at the playground out in front of the apartment when the phone rang.

"Mrs. Robertson, do you have a brother, Ralph Elmer?"

I was suddenly alert. My brother, Ralph, and his wife, Ginny, were visiting our parents in the Near East. Because of business commitments, I knew that Ralph was planning to fly back in a few days before Ginny.

"Yes," I said, "I do have a brother, but he's in Europe."

"He's on his way back, as a matter of fact, Mrs. Robertson. This is radio control calling from Idlewild Airport. Your brother's plane is over the Atlantic now and he has become ill. He will need medical attention as soon as the plane arrives."

I noted names and flight numbers and times, and then put down the receiver. I was fond of this tall, auburn-haired brother of mine. Older than I, he rarely had asked me to do anything for him, and I was glad to be able to help him out now. But I knew I couldn't handle the situation alone. I needed Pat's help, but I needed more than that. This was going to be an upsetting time.

As I stood there in the living room praying silently even before I called Pat to join me, I found myself in the middle of a strange experience. I asked the Lord to take complete control. While I was still praying, I suddenly felt as if I were walking through something the Lord knew all about. He would provide the answers *as* I needed them. All I had to do was move forward; He would do the supplying.

A surge of confidence swept over me. I didn't have to be afraid. I opened the window and called Pat; then, while he was gathering up toys, I phoned Ralph's doctor in Columbus, Ohio and reached him immediately. Everything went so smoothly that by the time Pat and the children came in, all had been arranged. We'd meet Ralph at Idlewild, then transfer him immediately to the next plane headed for Columbus.

"It was the most amazing experience, Pat," I said. "It was as if I didn't need to be in control at all."

Pat reached out and touched my cheek affectionately, his eyes all the while searching mine. He said quietly, "In my opinion that's what Christian self-control is all about, Honey. It's not a rigid, steel-like control of me by myself, but just the opposite—control of my self by God."

The events of the next day and a half seemed to run together. Pat and I decided that I'd have to stay in Columbus until things settled down. We would pack quickly and drive out and then Pat would drive back alone while I stayed to help out.

Thankfully Ralph's plane to New York was on time. We watched as an attendant brought him down the ramp in a wheelchair. Ralph tried to wave a greeting, but he was almost in tears from pain. We hugged and promised him that he wasn't going to be alone. An ambulance would take him to the hospital in Columbus. Ralph smiled. I soon had him aboard another plane, and Pat and the children and I started driving to Columbus.

Timmy and Elizabeth were quiet as they looked out the window; Gordon was asleep. I rested my head on the seat back, thinking about the change that had come into my life. I could scarcely believe what was happening to me. Here I was in the middle of a crisis and I was just flowing with it! It was almost as if the Lord had taken me into the two experiences of reacting to Bedford-Stuyvesant and reacting to Ralph's illness side by side to show me the difference between trying to control my self and allowing my self to be controlled by God.

It was early morning when I awoke, and to my great joy I saw that we were in the unmistakable surburban areas of Columbus—carefully tended lawns, neat shrubbery and well-cared-for homes. I felt safe here.

We turned a corner, and there was the English Tudor I knew so well. The minute the children spotted their grandparents' house they began squealing. Once unpacked, Pat went straight upstairs to rest since he'd driven most of the way and would be starting back to New York within hours. While I was calling the hospital to check on Ralph, the children scampered to their special hideaway upstairs, filled with games and dolls and toys. Ralph's condition, I learned, had been diagnosed as a kidney ailment, but he was "resting comfortably." I left word that I would be in soon to visit.

That night I went up to my room and remembered my "Secret Dream." In all the intervening years I had not forgotten one detail of that dream. Was it a preparation for what was about to happen? Perhaps so, at least in part. For the dream depicted a stripping away, and although I did not know it yet, within an incredibly short span of time most of the things I thought I owned would be firmly and not too gently stripped away.

While Pat was still sleeping, I took the DeSoto and went to visit Ralph. It was the first time I had been inside a hospital since I had stopped working. Just walking into the atmosphere made me feel at home. I sniffed the alcohol as if it were perfume, walked through the green halls with joy and had the urge to go comfort a weeping patient.

When I reached Ralph's room, he was asleep. Instinctively I checked his pulse. Ralph opened his eyes. "Hello, Dede."

"How are you feeling, Ralph?"

"A lot better now. Seems like everything is under control," Ralph said drowsily and closed his eyes. I kissed him and left.

When I told Pat that Ralph would be in the hospital for a couple of weeks, he suggested that he drive back to New York to do some serious praying about his next move. It sounded like a good idea. Pat would have the apartment to himself. He could also meet Ginny's plane when she arrived in New York and bring her up to date on all that was happening.

So, shortly, the children and I were kissing Pat goodby. We stood on the lawn waving until the blue DeSoto was out of sight. I had no idea, as I stood there, what I was going to face before I saw that car again.

Within a few days I was lulled into a comfortable routine, one that I followed closely for two weeks: visits to Ralph, shopping trips with old friends, lots of time to enjoy the kids. This is the way I'd like to live, I confessed to myself. I couldn't do what Barbara is doing.

Then one day the postman arrived with a letter from Pat. He told me he'd been praying a lot and asked about the children. At the end of the letter there was a line— almost as postscript—saying that the Lord had told him to follow Luke 12:33.

I didn't look up Luke 12:33. Pat was often guided by Scriptures and I was comfortable in trusting him again.

And so I sat down and wrote with full confidence, "Pat, do whatever the Lord tells you to do."

Ginny returned from Europe glad to find everything under control. One afternoon, shortly after answering Pat's letter, I went to Ralph and Ginny's house for a visit. At Ginny's invitation, I called home.

The phone in our apartment rang once, twice . . . I could hear the low hum of Ginny's refrigerator. Then the operator cut in to tell me that my call should be replaced to a number in Brooklyn.

"Brooklyn!" I exclaimed. I recognized Barbara and Dick's number!

I sat down heavily on the kitchen stool. As I dialed a second time, I could feel my face tightening. I've got to get hold of myself, I said almost aloud. This may not be what it seems . . .

"Hello, Barbara? It's Dede."

"Just a minute, Dede," Barbara said quickly. "I think you'd better talk to Pat."

"Pat, what's going on?"

"Well, Dede, I thought we agreed. In Luke 12:33 Jesus says to sell everything you own and give it to the poor. So I did."

I could not comprehend what he was saying. My head

suddenly developed a strange buzzing. *Get hold of yourself, Dede.*

"I don't think I quite understand, Pat," I managed to say in a voice not my own.

"Well, I put an ad in the paper. We had a big tag sale, and sold just about everything. Listen, Dede, you'll be happy to hear that Gen and Harald bought that living room set you recovered. You know they've always liked the blues in that set."

I said nothing at all.

"Well," Pat rushed on, "not everything went. The children's beds are still here, their toys, your pots and pans, your clothes, and I think I still have the candelabra, and of course, the car. But basically everything is gone and" his voice dropped, ". . . I gave up the apartment."

I can't believe this. It's not really happening. "The fish . . . did you sell the guppies too, Pat?"

"I gave them away." Pat's voice was subdued.

"Where do you expect to live?" I heard someone else's calm voice say, and I was surprised that it was mine. I was crying.

"Right here. For awhile anyhow. With Dick and Barbara."

I knew this would happen . . . I always knew it . . . and I can't take it . . . Lord. I was crying harder now. *You've got to take over now because there's no way I can handle this . . . take control . . . You be in control . . . Please help me.* The tears were rolling down my cheeks.

"Dede, are you there?"

"I'm here. And the money, Pat, did you give that away, too?"

"Most of it, yes. You know how strongly we've always felt about mission? Well. . . . " Pat's voice was very low indeed now. When again I said nothing, Pat changed the subject.

"I thought I'd drive out tomorrow to get you and the children. Then we'll go to Virginia to visit my mother. I'll tell all my friends about the things the Lord is doing in our lives."

"Drive-to-Lexington-to-visit-your-mother-that-sounds-very-nice—Pat," I said in a voice that reminded me of a robot.

"Gee, Dede, I'm glad you aren't angry. See you in a real short while now."

He hadn't heard me. I think it was the way he didn't understand my feelings that hurt me the most. I was trying not to slam down the receiver. *O God, I need Your strength.*

"Dede?" Pat's voice was saying. "Good-by."

I managed a muffled, "Good-by." As I sat there and looked at this spotless kitchen my mind flashed back to the grimy brownstone in Brooklyn—our new home.

"Dede what's wrong?" asked Ginny from the doorway.

"Oh nothing, really," I said. I was trying so hard to be a "witness"! I knew I hadn't fooled Ginny, but she didn't press me.

That evening I could barely get through dinner. I was not too enthusiastic when I told the children Daddy was coming in a day or so. When they finally went to sleep, I stumbled into my own room, where I'd had the "Secret Dream." I stood at the French casement windows, looking out. I could see the street—everything here was so clean and well-kept. The leaves on the trees with their silvery hue touched by the moonlight were a lush, summer green. The stars twinkled more brightly than in New York. The streets were empty and quiet; I could hear

only the sound of the katydids rubbing their wings together. I went to bed and tried to pray. But my prayers
were interrupted by thoughts of whether or not I should
just tell Pat to go on without us.

*Oh, Pat, I am so tempted to leave you. Thank God
for this trip to Lexington. It's my only hope. Perhaps
someone—your mother, a friend, a relative, anyone—will
talk sense into you. Lord, please help me out of this.
Please, Lord, I have to trust You.*

I spent the next day washing and ironing clothes and
straightening out the house. The following day I heard
Tim and Elizabeth shouting "Daddy, Daddy!" I picked
up Gordon and walked over to the front door. In the
drive was the old blue DeSoto—one of our few possessions, now. Pat got down on the grass to listen to Elizabeth
and Tim both trying to talk to him at the same time.

He waited outside and looked at me still standing in
the doorway holding Gordon. His expression said, "I'm
stalling, Dede. I've had time to think about how this must
have hit you, and I don't know what to say."

And so I walked slowly over to him. Pat took my hand
in his and we walked toward the house. There was so
very little I could say about the tag sale, so I told him
that Ralph was home sooner than expected and doing
well. At the door Pat stopped.

"I'm really sorry, Sweetheart," he said, as if we were
in the middle of a conversation. "I *thought* we had
agreed. It seems impulsive to you because you weren't
there. But I spent a great many hours in prayer before
I wrote you. I kept getting the same word: 'Sell all you
have and give it to the poor.' "

"But everything, Pat? Everything? It's all gone?"

"No, Dede. I've stored a few things in the basement
of the manse. Dick helped me build a platform and we
stacked everything on it. A good thing, too, because that

same night it poured, and the basement flooded. But our things were dry."

The more he talked the more he was convinced that it had all worked out beautifully. *Well, Lord. I'm really going to have to trust You. I'm going to start right now by asking You to heal my hurt. I need You to control my emotions.*

Pat said he'd like to get started for Lexington after he had had a little rest. While he was sleeping I called Ginny to thank her for her hospitality and to say goodby.

"I hope everything works out for you, Dede."

All I could say was, "I hope so, too, Ginny. I'm going to have to trust the Lord."

The shortest, most direct route to Lexington from Columbus that sunny day in late summer, 1959, took us through side roads, winding roads and bad roads. There were not nearly enough big trucks to satisfy the children. With little to hold their attention, they kept shouting at Pat from the back seat. They told him in their high-pitched children's voices about how much they loved walking to the drugstore during their stay in Columbus, and about how they were getting to be the best baseball players in all of Ohio, and about how much cake they ate.

Gordon fell asleep in his car seat, his pudgy leg twisted under him. I reached over and straightened it out. The car grew quiet and I used the occasion to try to sort out my thoughts. Slowly I became aware of a sense of calm settling over me which I couldn't explain. Here we were planning to live in that dreadful area of Brooklyn, yet I felt at peace, as if my *emotions* knew, although my mind didn't, that things were under control. Was the Lord changing me?

Just then we passed a sign saying we were entering Lexington, Virginia. Everyone was excited as Pat pointed out landmarks from his childhood: a vacant lot, a duck pond, the site of an exciting fire.

Then we were at Pat's home. The Robertsons' house was large and formal, built in the style of a French manor house. It was an even greater contrast to Bedford-Stuyvesant than my parents' home.

Pat's father was in Washington, but his mother must have been watching for us, because she was at the door when we pulled up. This beautiful, slightly plump, silver-haired southern lady, was almost dancing in her joy at seeing Pat and his family. She stood on tip-toe to kiss her tall son and gave me a one-armed hug as she encircled our prattling children with the other. Then we trooped up the curved walk, fashioned of bricks laid in a colonial pattern, and almost immediately went in to dinner.

In spite of my travel-weariness, dinner was a delight. The children behaved well and Gordon spilled his milk only once. Our conversation dealt mainly with remembrances of Pat's growing up in the house, his old classmates, what the senator had been doing.

The children knew that Grandmommy Robertson would pamper them, and they were right. But a stimulating thing happened the next day to Pat and me too.

By the time I had come down for breakfast on the terrace the following morning, the household was in a state of excitement. I served myself some orange juice. Timmy could hardly contain himself.

"Daddy's going to be on the radio!" he exclaimed.

I blinked and looked questioningly at Pat, but it was his mother who explained.

"Do you remember the church that wanted Pat to preach while their pastor is away? Well, now they're asking him to take the pastor's daily radio show, too."

I looked inquiringly at Pat again. He nodded. "That's right. Fifteen minutes a day for a week. I should be nervous but I'm not. It's as if it were the most natural thing in the world—going on radio."

"Well, we'll all be listening," I said, surprised at my own excitement. "If you're awful, we'll keep it a secret."

That afternoon we all gathered in the Robertsons' living room to listen to Pat on the radio. He was really good. His voice had an air of assurance; he was urbane and witty and well versed on the Bible. I knew it wasn't just wifely pride when I told Pat that evening at dinner, "Pat, you were very, very natural. This is a side of you I didn't know existed."

Then something else happened. Before we left Lexington, a letter came to Pat's mother from an old family friend named George Lauderdale who lived in the Tidewater area of the state. In the postscript (it's amazing how many of life's big events come in a P.S.) George mentioned that there was a television station for sale in Portsmouth, Virginia. George wondered if Pat would be interested in claiming Channel 27 for the Lord?

We chuckled at the thought. The whole episode was refreshing. It felt good to laugh. My spirits lifted. "Claiming a station for the Lord; he means buying it, doesn't he, Pat?"

"Yes, I would say so, Dede."

"And after the great tag sale we don't have one hundred dollars to our name!" I said, still amused.

Pat was laughing, too.

"We certainly don't know anything about running a television station," he added.

"We don't even *own* a television set," Tim said, a little bitterly.

Then suddenly Pat grew serious. "Yet there's some-

thing strange going on," he said. "I'm asked to speak
on radio for the first time in my life. Then I'm asked to
buy a television station."

I was amazed to see how interested Pat seemed, in
spite of our lighthearted attitude.

Shortly, we began packing for the trip back to New
York. It was an odd time, deliberately leaving this gracious lifestyle for heaven only knew what.

Leaving Lexington was quite a different experience
from leaving Columbus. I was not afraid. By yielding myself to Him, God was teaching me that when I no longer
tried to control my own life, then He gave me a sense
that life was under control.

What had been fear was slowly, slowly being translated
into adventure.

GOODNESS MEAT LOAF

When the larder is bare, this dish does wonders.

2½ cups ground soybeans	2 t Worcestershire sauce
1 t salt	¼ cup chopped green
½ cup bread crumbs	pepper (optional)
½ cup tomato sauce	1 t dried mustard
½ onion, chopped	1 egg, beaten
½ t pepper	

Mix together and place in greased loaf pan. Bake in 350° oven for one hour. For company, or when available, substitute ½ cup ground beef for ½ cup soybeans. Garnish with tomato wedges or mushrooms for last ½ hour of baking. Serves six.

5

GOODNESS

THERE ARE TIMES when God puts us into a crucible and then turns the heat up to 3,000 degrees. When this happens He does a great deal for us in an incredibly short period of time.

The moment of our departure finally came. The sun was just breasting the tree tops as Grandmommy Robertson saw us all into the old DeSoto which we had packed the night before. The children stood around drowsily. I knew they would fall asleep again just as soon as we were on the highway. Pat tenderly said good-by to his mother, we waved, honked twice and were on our way.

I took the first stint that day while Pat and the children slept. It was a good thing, too, for otherwise I might not have turned on the car radio, softly, and heard the preacher. He spoke in a drawl, and sometimes his grammar was faulty, but what he said was to play an important role in my life over the next two months.

"What we've got to do," the preacher was saying, "is refocus on the positive. Deliberately choose the positive. It's all Biblical! Whatsoever things are true, honest, and

79

just, pure, lovely and of good report. Think on these
things, the Bible says in Philippians 4:8."

Well, that was just what I needed that morning. I held
onto the verse all the while the children and Pat slept,
then through our first rest stop and through the traffic
of Baltimore when the children began to bombard Pat
with questions about our new home in the Bedford-Stuyvesant section of Brooklyn. That was when the Bible verse
became especially useful. *Whatsover things are of good
report, Lord, those are the things I will focus on.*

The children were curious about who else was living
in the house in Brooklyn.

"You remember Mr. Simmons?" Pat began, in answer.
"Well, he and his wife Barbara are sort of in charge of
the house. They have a new baby, Mary Elizabeth, that
you're all going to like. And there's another lady there,
too, someone your mother and I knew at seminary—Alice
Blair. And there's a man from Jamaica. And there's a
younger man who has a physical problem and sometimes
his girl friend comes over for meals."

I was as curious as the children. For heaven's sakes, I
wondered, where will everyone sleep so that we can have
some privacy? When I had visited this big old manse
before, I hadn't paid much attention to where people
slept; I was too busy being astonished at how dirty Gordon
got in just a few moments of crawling around.

We approached the skyline of New York City just as
hot-under-the-collar motorists were honking and cursing
their various ways across the George Washington Bridge
while we forged past them in the opposite direction. Then
our tired old car crossed the shimmering South Bronx,
an infernal cauldron on that terribly sticky September
late afternoon.

As we negotiated the cluttered, clanging streets that
were funneling us across the city toward Brooklyn, I be-

gan to get nervous all over again. But the children in their playsuits chattered and pointed out the open car windows, peppering Pat and me with their excited commentary about the tall buildings, the strolling couples, the new smells. Surely the city appeals most to people who don't have their focus set on fear, I mused, and my Bible passage replayed itself inside my head, ". . . whatsoever things are lovely, whatsoever things are of good report . . . think on these things."

Within half an hour we had gone down the East Side Drive of Manhattan, crossed the Brooklyn Bridge and were approaching our new home on Classon Avenue. People in skimpy clothes were sitting outside on the sidewalk, fanning themselves or hanging out of open windows. Some were stretched out in the gutter, probably passed out from alcohol or drugs.

Now even Timmy and Elizabeth and Gordon were more watchful. They observed other children playing in the streets. But these were not red-haired, blue-eyed boys and girls in bright, relatively clean sunsuits. The street kids of Brooklyn were mostly black or Hispanic. They had hollow eyes and bored expressions. Their toys were the refuse of the streets—beer cans, sticks, hubcaps torn from car wheels. Instinctively I pushed the lock button on my car door.

Then Pat pulled up to the manse at 33 Classon. I was filled with numbness. Could *this* be God's perfect provision for those who had given Him their hearts and their lives! Pat tooted the horn. He was smiling and relaxed. "Well, kids, this is it," he said.

"We're going to live here, Daddy?" Elizabeth asked, but there was no judgment in her tone.

In a moment Dick Simmons came out to greet us. Behind him appeared Barbara. They ran down the steps of the brownstone to the street. To see such friendly faces in the midst of this alien environment was a tremendous encouragement to me. We hugged and kissed and all talked at once, but I kept looking over my shoulder to make sure that our children were safe.

After Barbara and I had greeted each other, Dick and Pat took the older children by their hands to show them the main floor. Barbara and I followed behind as we went through the parlor and dining room. Gordon, at one year, wanted to walk, but I wouldn't let him. Not just yet.

"This place looks so good now," Barbara said. "You won't believe it. The parishioners have it all cleaned up."

The house was just as I remembered it, except that now, after all the painting and cleaning, the whole effect was more cheerful. Things echo in this place, I thought, and most of all the laughter. "Whatsoever things are true . . . " I couldn't wait to go up to our floor. We would probably have the second or maybe the third floor to ourselves for privacy, since ours was the largest family in the household.

Then I saw freckle-faced, sandy-haired Alice Blair coming from the back of the house, and my heart leaped happily. I remembered how Alice had said she felt the Lord was calling her to Brooklyn and here she was! Right behind her another friendly face appeared. "Dick!" Pat called out and ran to embrace still another seminary friend, Dick White. Dick's finely-defined features broke into a smile.

"Now we can pick up where we left off in Queens," he joked. Together we went downstairs to inspect the communal prayer room and the kitchen. The redecoration hadn't quite reached this level; the kitchen was just as dark and dank as before. When Dick flicked on the ghostly ceiling light, a dozen cockroaches darted for cover. But Pat didn't seem to notice.

"Before we do any more looking around," I said, perhaps a little hurriedly, "I'd better get the children upstairs and show them our rooms."

Again Pat said nothing. He just started upstairs, holding Tim's and Elizabeth's hands. I trudged behind heavily with Gordon still in my arms. Halfway up the bare staircase, Pat casually mentioned that Dick and Barbara Simmons and Dick White had the second floor for their rooms and offices.

"Oh, then we get the third floor?" I asked.

"Well, not exactly, Sweetheart, but I know you're going to like it here."

On the third floor, to the left, was Alice's room. The door was open and we looked in. There were two youth beds and a small single bed crowded into the garret, which made me wonder a bit. But Pat was already turning away from Alice's room, talking. He pointed out that the tiny room at the end of the hall was occupied by the Jamaican and, on occasion, by the young man who was spastic. Then Pat stepped across the dark, bare hall and opened a door. He stood back. So I walked through, into an average sized, very hot room painted a pale, pastel green and sporting dotted Swiss curtains at the one window.

"Well, this is it, Dede. Our room."

Our room? I couldn't speak. There were five of us in our family.

"*One* of our rooms," Pat corrected himself. "Alice offered to take all three kids, but she didn't have enough space. So we'll have Gordon with us," he said, pointing to a crib crowded into one corner. "Darling, you've got to understand this is a communal house. Everyone shares here."

Without saying a word at all I stepped to the window and looked down into the neighbor's litter-filled back yard. In spite of myself I was remembering Columbus and the trees which I could see from the casement windows in my room there. I felt Pat come over and stand beside me.

"I'm sure it must be tough, Dede. But I just know the Lord means us to be here. At least for a short while."

Well, I said to myself, *whatsover things are true . . .*

Before I had a chance to go any further I heard Timmy and Elizabeth giggling outside our door. I wiped my eyes and walked past Pat into the hall. Timmy was hanging over the railing and Elizabeth was at his side jumping up and down like a cheerleader, shouting, "Try again, try again!"

Incredibly, as I watched, Tim spit down the stairwell.

"Timmy! What are you doing! Stop that immediately."

"But then I won't hit it," he said.

"What on earth are you talking about?" Pat asked, coming out of the room.

"I was trying to hit the bottom step," Timmy said, "but I can only get to about the tenth one." His eyes ran quickly between Pat and me. "Okay, I'll stop," he said.

Suddenly Pat couldn't be the stern father any longer. With a smile he said to me, "See, Honey? Our family's going to be lively no matter where we live. True?"

He took Tim and Elizabeth by the hand and led them downstairs, calling back to me that I should try to put Gordon down and get a nap myself. I tried to push the window open, but it got stuck halfway with decades of well-intended redecoration. I put Gordon in his crib where he collapsed, then I collapsed, too, on the sagging, squeaky bed and waited quietly for Gordon's sighs to tell me he had gone to sleep. I lay there staring at the pastel paint above my head. It was already beginning to peel and I wondered if this was the kind of paint with lead in it.

Then my ears began to pick up the new sounds I would be living with. From the Jamaican's room, a raucous ca-

lypso music began to play; from inside the wall behind
my head came a scurrying noise; there was the dull roar
of the city outside—cars, shouts, rumbling trucks, barking
dogs; and, incredibly, from the floors below, the gentle
sound of laughter.

This was so odd, I thought. Here I was feeling the defeat
of the ghetto seeping into my pores. To be honest, this
place was gruesome. There were rats everywhere. There
were bugs and roaches all over the place. Yet at the same
time I knew that in Christ I could live on an island of
goodness. I could experience that goodness even now,
but I would have to work at it. It was not going to come
to me, I would have to seek it.

I awoke, still exhausted. It was nighttime. Pat had put
Tim and Elizabeth to bed across the hall. I went down
for a late snack, said hello to the others briefly and went
back to bed where I collapsed again. The next morning
I awoke to find Pat already dressed, tip-toeing around.
"Where are you going?" I asked, looking at my watch;
it was almost eight o'clock.

"Dede, I'm sure you know this; I mean, I did tell you
didn't I? There is a routine in this household. From five
to six, there is a prayer and worship service. Then from
six to seven we wait upon the Spirit to give us direction.
Then there is intercessory prayer. Breakfast is at eight.
Do you want to join us for breakfast?"

I was sorry I'd slept through the prayer time even
though I didn't particularly like the idea of being slotted
into a schedule. But I got the children up and we all
traipsed down the three flights of stairs to the basement-
kitchen. The children could barely wait to get to breakfast. I'm sure they expected to smell bacon, and to hear
eggs crackling in a frying pan.

"What do we eat?" Tim whispered to me, looking at
the empty kitchen table.

"Whatever there is," I said hesitantly.

Just then the staff—the Simmonses, Dick White, Alice Blair and Pat—came into the kitchen and we all sat down at the oilcloth-covered door-table on its spindly legs. After he said grace, Dick Simmons cut slices of a hard molasses bread for everyone.

Barbara added a powdered orange juice substitute to a pitcher of water.

"Meals are simple here," she said as Timmy and Elizabeth looked at the slices of bread on their plates. "Most of our money is spent on missions."

Tim wasn't interested. He wrinkled his nose, sniffed a few times. "What's that?" he asked Alice, pointing toward the stove.

I knew immediately what it was.

"Soybeans," Alice replied. "We eat them almost every day. Along with a lot of blackstrap molasses and onions and day-old bread." Alice looked at Barbara, her eyes laughing, from which I gathered that our household was heavily into these foods. Timmy didn't find the conversation humorous at all.

"Tonight we're having soybeans with rutabagas," Barbara advised. I had to blink when she said that because I couldn't think of any way that soybeans could improve the taste of turnip-like rutabagas! "The men call the dish our 'Tribulation food,'" Barbara added, laughing again. It was the first—but certainly wasn't to be the last—time I heard the idea that soybeans would be one of God's main resources during the Tribulation which is so graphically described in the Bible. For a fleeting moment my memory flashed back to my "Secret Dream." We had food and water stored up in the cellar during that turbulent time. Could the food have been soybeans?

"There are lots of good soybean recipes in my cookbooks," I said, coming back to the present. "Unless Pat sold the cookbooks too." I gave Pat a sideways glance and he assured me we'd go look at the remnants of our belongings after breakfast.

So a few minutes later Pat and Dick Simmons and I went down to the dim dungeon where our goods were stored. There, resting, on the wooden platform Dick and Pat had made, was everything we owned. A few textbooks and cookbooks, the silver candelabra, Tim's tricycle, our old Boston rocker, the English pram Mother had given me, a few pots and pans. By some miracle I was able to keep from crying. Was it simply that I'd already gone through the emotion of the tag sale, or was it that I had determined to keep my eye focused on the good in life, as the Bible told me to do?

Pat and Dick took the tricycle through the iron-gated basement door and up the steps to the sidewalk. I wanted to see the church but I wasn't yet sure how I was supposed to act in this neighborhood and asked Pat whether or not I should take the children down alone.

Pat answered carefully. Our particular street was not as bad as some, he said, but gangs were a problem anywhere in Bedford-Stuyvesant. Dick agreed. We shouldn't test God with foolhardiness, but neither should we be afraid to go about our work.

"Which adds up to two things, Dede," Pat said. "First we have to be sure we are about His business. And then we have to trust Him to protect us while we are on that business."

I had no problem with that. I knew that the Lord must care intensely for the pain and injustice of Bedford-Stuyvesant and that He must want His church to be here. I might resist Bedford-Stuyvesant with a part of me (who wouldn't?), but I was also enraged at the Satan-inspired circumstances that reduced people to this! So, standing there on the sidewalk, Pat and Dick and I asked the Lord to give us His protection whenever we went out. Then

the men waved good-by and our children and I set off
for our first encounter with our neighbors.

We paraded down the sidewalk—Timmy on his tricycle, Elizabeth walking beside me, Gordon in his stroller.
Tim pedaled furiously. He rang his bell often and waved
heartily to the children he met. The slum kids did not
return Tim's greetings, but Tim wasn't daunted at all.

That evening I had my first chance to feed our commune one of my somewhat more interesting soy dishes.
Joining the staff at the table were the Jamaican, his spastic
friend Philip, Philip's pregnant girl friend, and an older
black woman named Ruby who, before she became a
Christian, had been the madam at a brothel that used
to operate next door.

When we were all seated and had asked the blessing,
I pushed my chair back and went to the oven. The soybean dish I served (instead of the rutabaga monstrosity
that had been planned) was my "Goodness Meat Loaf."
It was, I had to admit, not bad. I was pleased to notice
that there was none left at the end of the meal. Perhaps
the real secret of preparing soy dishes is to disguise the
little bean.

Over the next week my role in our hectic commune
began to become clearer. My primary responsibility was
to care for my own three children. But I also had an
important role in the kitchen, not only helping to prepare
meals but also using information I had picked up at Yale
and in Queens about cheap, tasty, nutritious meals. Each
of us on staff required plenty of high-energy protein to
do the work set before us. But we also needed energy
to help us face the emotions of living together. For there
definitely was no sweetness-and-light atmosphere around
our slum commune. We didn't need dragged-down bodies to add to the natural conflict.

And there *was* conflict. Our children were without a safe and interesing place in which to play. The backyard was solid hard-packed dirt, with dust constantly blowing off the top; there was not a blade of grass anywhere. The children tried playing in that yard but soon gave up; there was nothing they could do on that hardpan. So as often as possible I made an escape—to a park, a library, a museum, a friend who lived far away. People in the commune didn't appreciate my being away so much.

Then, paradoxically, there was a desire to be out on the streets, working. I wanted to be with our neighbors more often, for I was beginning to find them kind and generous, but working outside of our immediate neighborhood made Pat nervous. Perhaps the worst cause of tension was the line of authority that had been set up in the house. I sometimes thought Dick and Barbara Simmons assumed more authority than was their right, but they reminded me that it was the group decision, not their own, that put them in charge here. There were conflicts in the kitchen, too. We women were supposed to work together, but often we didn't see eye to eye about spending a little extra money to make some dish more palatable.

In short it was a slum commune and there wasn't anything romantic about it at all.

With all the tension built into this situation, I knew we would be better off if we ate high-energy food, for experiments show that whenever tension mounts, the body calls for more protein. We all needed to understand the importance of a good fuel supply for our bodies. So during the next several days I found chances to get in a little propaganda. Soybeans was my subject. Soy flour, I said, as I served the delicious "Love Waffles" that everyone enjoyed, is a giant among protein foods. The problem is to get people even to try soybeans because they seem so unglamorous.

"We ought to take a lesson from the commercial world," I said to the table, passing around another stack of waffles. "Mix soybeans with something else. That's the key. In the commercial world we're eating soybeans all the time and liking them too. In soups and puddings and candy and pastas and baking mixes."

That was enough for the moment. Tim had finished and was making pathways through the syrup on his plate with an uneaten bite of waffle. So I changed the subject, excused the children, and helped with the cleaning up.

But not before I'd said a flash prayer.

Thank You, Lord, for what You are showing us. Not just about healthy and cheap eating, but about Yourself. You do care about what we eat. You do supply us with the means to stay healthy, whether or not we have fat pocketbooks.

So it was that our new life began in the foreign place called Bedford-Stuyvesant. Over the weeks that followed we all worked extremely hard. On the face of it, the ministry was having little impact. Attendance at church did not rise dramatically in spite of ardent street preaching and social-action projects. There was little visible healing of deep-seated separations. Blacks still preferred the company of blacks, Jews wanted to be with Jews, the Hispanic people with others who spoke Spanish. But in spite of continual discouragements, there was an underlying sense that God had His own reasons for our being there. Sometimes I suspected that being in Bedford-Stuyvesant was, in God's eyes, an exercise in obedience for us. I suspected that He had other plans for meeting the needs of the ghetto, since our efforts seemed to get such mediocre results. Perhaps in some mysterious way, being

in Bedford-Stuyvesant was more for our own benefit than
for those we had come to serve. Perhaps He had some
other plans for each of us but wanted us to identify first
with the reality of suffering.

In the midst of all the ministry and the daily coping
with poverty, Pat began to do an interesting thing. He
started to talk a lot about television. He referred often
to George Lauderdale's suggestion that we buy the Portsmouth station.

"Do you think . . ." he kept asking us all in a dozen
different ways, ". . . do you think that suggestion could
possibly be from God?"

MEEKNESS BITS

Perks up salads with unique flavor

1 cup mashed cooked
   soybeans
2 T Liquid Smoke
1 T Tender Quick
food coloring: 8 drops
   yellow, 6 red, 2 green

1 T corn oil
1 T Tang
1 t Fruit Fresh, powdered (a
   Vitamin C used in canning
   & freezing)
1 t brown sugar

    Mix all ingredients together and then line cookie sheet with aluminum foil. Spread nectar thickly over foil. Bake at 225° at least 3 hours. Mixture must be completely dry. Let cool and peel away foil and crumble into bits. Use in salads and other dishes as a homemade variety of bacon bits.

6

MEEKNESS

OVER THE WEEKS I was slowly learning to adjust to living in a room and a half, with soybeans and wilted vegetables as the staples in our diet. The vegetables came from the wholesale markets in Manhattan. At dawn each morning after prayer time, one of the men went down to the markets to buy food that had not sold. If it was my day to cook I never knew whether my vegetables for the day were going to be soggy onions, bruised tomatoes or wilted, browned lettuce.

I still felt ill at ease. It wasn't just the ghetto that bothered me, with its screams in the night, its blowing trash, acrid smells and vermin. What bothered me even more was the old problem of friction in our own household here at the manse.

Oh, my frustration wasn't as bad as it had once been. I did see progress whenever I kept my eye focused on whatsoever-things-are-good. For the most part that technique was helping me adjust to my surroundings. But when it came to *people* I was still bridling.

Whenever Barbara and I disagreed about a menu, or

93

Dick and I about schedules, or whenever Ben, the Jamaican, sang too loudly or Ruby stayed in the bathroom too
long, or anyone at all ordered me to do something—
whenever such events occurred, my old rebelliousness
emerged. In short I was out of step with the rest of the
commune. It's a wonder the others put up with me at
all.

One night when Pat and I were alone in our bedroom
I asked, "Do you think the Lord wants us to stay here
forever?"

"Why do you ask, Dede?"

"Oh, I don't know, it's just that I feel so inadequate.
I sit there at meals and hear you and Dick White and
the others telling your exciting stories. I just don't feel
I'm contributing."

"Now, Honey, of course you are . . ."

"You're not hearing me out, Pat. My problem is I don't
even feel that I *want* to get intimately involved with
this commune. It scares me. I feel like I might get gobbled
up."

"I know," Pat said softly, taking my hand in the dark.
"Sometimes I feel threatened, too. I think God is hum-
bling us, Dede. We've got to understand more about being totally yielded. Frankly, Dede, I find that difficult."

"And so," I said into the night, "do I."

Occasionally we still found ourselves talking about the
television station down in Virginia. Even thinking about
it seemed like a fantasy. How would we ever find the
money to buy a television station when Pat was going
down to the market to scrounge day-old vegetables? Nevertheless Pat kept raising questions. Could television ever
be of God? Wasn't it an evil force, really? On the other
hand, why should we just turn over the whole of television
to the world, the flesh and the devil?

One evening at dinner I made the mistake of asking

Pat if he were considering television as a ministry. His reaction was instantaneous.

"Dede, I don't know anything about TV." And then the real problem slipped out. "Besides . . ." Pat started to finish his sentence, then stopped. His next gesture said everything. His arm swept over the table—past Ruby, past the Jamaican and the spastic boy. His gesture went on to include the neighborhood and all we were trying to do here. It embraced the dispossessed men and women and their children, the teen-age prostitutes, the bright minds deadened with alcohol and drugs.

I knew what Pat meant, and so did the silent others at the table. The unspoken thought was in all our minds: What kind of Christian could abandon ministering in person to that boy who was stabbed on our street last week, in favor of a nice, safe, remote-controlled TV ministry?

And so the subject was dropped. I understood Pat right away. Our community really was trying to contribute to the neighborhood. Every one of us, including the children, was making a personal statement. Dick and Barbara found that their son, Paul, with all his motor awkwardness, was an instant link to others in the neighborhood. Black and Puerto Rican mothers would stop and talk with Barbara when she was out with Paul, because they shared a link of suffering and were outsiders too.

Our own Elizabeth was always inviting the neighborhood children to come home with her, which of course made it possible for me to know the children's mothers.

And Tim, with his tricycle, was the neighborhood hero. After that first day when I went with the children to the church, I had been giving Tim more and more freedom. I was growing accustomed to hearing a rap at the front door of the manse and opening it to see two or three of Tim's boy friends from the neighborhood stand-

ing on the steps asking if he could come out and bring
"the airplane," as they called Tim's tricycle.

In its own way, the "airplane" became a sacrifice. Tim
freely shared his tricycle with his friends and since there
were so many boys and only one tricycle, they developed
the technique of riding it two or three at a time. When
that happened the tricycle mysteriously became an airplane. With Tim in the pilot's seat, there might be a
Puerto Rican navigator riding on the handlebars and a
black tail gunner standing on the platform at the rear.

Tim wouldn't hear me when I suggested that his tricycle wasn't meant to carry well over a hundred pounds
of bounding, jostling boys. One bright, sunny fall day,
as I was sitting in the parlor window where I could watch
Tim and at the same time read Gordon a story, I heard
the slap of small feet on the sidewalk and saw Tim come
up the steps.

I went to the door carrying Gordon and there was Tim,
dirt-covered and tear-streaked. He was knuckling his eyes
as he gasped out the sad tidings.

"My airplane, Mommy! It's wrecked. It came apart
down the street."

Still carrying Gordon, I went down the steps and
started up the block. Sure enough, Timmy's tricycle had
made its last stand. The front wheel and handlebars were
in one place, the rear wheels and axle were in another.
Timmy's subdued and silent friends were sitting on the
curb, forlornly playing with the remnants.

"It's broken for good, isn't it, Mommy?"

"I'm afraid its beyond repair, Tim, yes."

"The whole thing just fell apart," Tim said. The other
boys nodded their brown heads in agreement.

"Well, I guess you just won't have a tricycle anymore,
Tim," I said. There was no money to buy a new one.

"No, you've got it wrong, Mommy. *They* won't have
a tricycle any more. And they're my *friends.*"

Right then, God revealed a truth to me. As Tim and Gordon and I started back to the manse, leaving the treasured tricycle as one more mound of flotsam on the streets of Bedford-Stuyvesant, I saw something I had never seen before. There was power in this kind of dynamic meekness. Tim was living by Matthew 18:3-4, "Unless you turn and become like children, you will never enter the kingdom of heaven. Whoever humbles himself like this child, he is the greatest in the kingdom of heaven."

For days Pat and some of the others in our household had been trying to persuade me to be baptized in water. Every morning we gathered in the large family room in the basement, next to the kitchen. This room with its overstuffed furniture and its small windows set high in the wall, was where we held our devotions. And it was here that the pressure was applied to me to be baptized. Pat's position was that baptism by complete immersion was not necessary to salvation, but that since Jesus set the example, we should follow. It was a steady campaign, not only from him but from others too, and one that I didn't appreciate.

Then one day in mid-October I learned that there was a baptismal party and picnic planned for the coming Saturday out on Long Island Sound.

Right away I sensed the plot. But to end the pressure I agreed to go along. "I really don't want you or Harald to baptize me, Pat," I announced. "Paul Morris, perhaps, but not you or Harald!"

Pat agreed. So on a bright, cheerful Saturday morning we all put on bathing suits under our street clothes and caravaned toward the north shore of Long Island to a warm, sandy private beach. Ruby was with us and Ben and Philip and a dozen other people. Paul Morris, as it turned out, had not been immersed himself. So he could not baptize me after all. In the end, as a point of deliberately yielding my own will to Pat's authority "as unto the Lord," (as the Bible puts it) I turned Gordon over to a friend, then prepared to be baptized. I stepped out of my street clothes, put on my black baptismal robes, and found myself wading out into the warm, salty water. Feeling more than a little self-conscious, I stepped forward and surrendered myself into Harald's and Pat's arms. They leaned me back into the water, baptizing me in the name of the Father, the Son and the Holy Ghost.

I came up out of the water completely wet, my hair dripping into my eyes. We all waded back to the beach for a communion service.

Suddenly the whole world was turning to gold. What was happening? Everything around me was bathed in color. The sky was still blue, but it had a patina of gold over it. The clouds were white, but they were white through a glowing gold. Trees were not autumn-colored but gold. I blinked hard. The gold still shone everywhere. There was a quality of peace over everyone, everything, as if I were no longer in charge. From that moment on, I felt, whatever happened to me was all right, because God was in charge.

I didn't want to break the moment. The glory continued. I didn't want to speak to anyone, and since others seemed to be in the same mood, I was able to remain in my own special cocoon of wonder. Then Harald asked if anyone wanted to receive the Baptism in the Holy Spirit. And I did! Oh, how I knew I wanted to receive this experience, too—if in fact there was any difference at all between the Baptism in the Holy Spirit and this transcendent, golden moment that was still happening to me.

But just at that moment I spotted Gordon toddling happily toward the water of Long Island Sound. I looked quickly to see if his sitter was running to catch him. She was nowhere near the child. So of course I took out after my little boy. When I scooped him away from the edge of the water and returned to the group, the special moment had passed. And so had the gold.

But I didn't mind. I never have thought of myself as a mystic, so I couldn't have held onto the mystery of that moment anyhow. I'm afraid that's just the way it is.

That night in our tiny bedroom, Pat asked me if I had enjoyed the day.

"Oh, yes. Yes, I did that."

"Did anything special happen?"

I told Pat about the golden world. He was intrigued. Was this the Baptism in the Holy Spirit? I thought so but Pat wasn't sure; I hadn't spoken in tongues.

But one thing was certain. I had just experienced the results of deliberately following the injunction of Ephesians 5:22: "Wives, submit yourselves unto your own husbands, as unto the Lord." The yielding had a peculiar rightness about it. Once I let go of insisting on my own way I saw the world as I had never seen it before, full of golden glory.

Almost immediately however the experience was repeated at another dimension.

We had been in Brooklyn for about two months now. It seemed to me that we'd been there much longer because enormous spiritual events were taking place in my life. I began attending a Bible study class with Alice and Dick White. The teacher, wouldn't you know it, spent a great deal of time talking about the Baptism in the Holy Spirit. He wanted to know how many of us had been filled with the Holy Spirit. After the experience on the beach I raised my hand.

"And how many of you," the teacher then asked, "speak in tongues?"

Here, I did not raise my hand.

"Because," the teacher went on, "anytime we feel we have been filled with the Spirit of God, we need to act on that belief. Your spiritual language is not of critical importance," he said, "but it is a wonderful gift and if you've been filled with the Spirit, you *should* be able to speak in tongues. Go home, kneel down and tell the Lord how much you love Him. Then begin to praise Him in the language He gives you."

An hour later I climbed the stairs at the manse, said good-night to Dick and Alice and opened the door to our little room. Pat and Gordon were asleep, their forms very still in the wan light that came in from the street.

Without waiting to get into my night clothes, I knelt beside the bed. I did just as the teacher had suggested and began to praise the Lord. I thanked Him for my wonderful family, for good health, for enough to eat and for our freedom to worship Him. While I was praying, just as naturally as if I were speaking in my own language, I began to pray in the Spirit. The tongue sounded like beautiful French to me, but it wasn't *my* French, for sure. My French was anything but beautiful.

Pat woke up. When he heard me praying in the Spirit he got out of bed and knelt beside me. I asked him if he would pray with me. This must have thrilled Pat as much as my praying in tongues, for it was the very first time I had ever asked him to pray with me.

When we came to a pause I told him once again about the golden beach experience. Pat listened in delight and in awe.

Over the next several mornings in our basement quiet time I tried to sort out all that was happening to me. One thing I knew for sure: after I'd agreed to follow Pat's leadership in the matter of water baptism, changes began. A rebelliousness that I'd noted in my makeup seemed to be melting. In the past I'd always told myself Pat could do his thing and I could do my thing. If tensions got bad enough I could always go back to Columbus and raise the children in my parents' home, supporting them with my income as a registered nurse. But now I knew that I could not, in fact, leave Pat. I had a relationship with him that was like Christ's relationship to the Church. We were mystically bound together; it would be like leaving the Lord Himself if I broke up the marriage.

Neither Pat nor I yet understood that this was a preparation time in the eyes of the Lord. God knew that we would soon need to be a true team as never before. I had surrendered my own natural authority to Pat, the authority that comes because I am a capable and well-trained woman. As soon as that surrender occurred, we became a team.

Not that I rolled over and played doormat. I doubt that this could ever be what the Lord means by submitting. It was, rather, a recognition that divided authority leads to chaos. So I gave my authority to Pat as unto the Lord. In doing so of course there was risk, because Pat is very capable indeed of making mistakes. But I trusted that the Lord would honor this yielding. Since He ordered it, He would protect us all from our errors and would allow us to thrive in the new relationship.

But the Lord was not yet through with using our time in Brooklyn.

One day Pat dropped a bomb into my emotions.

"Sweetheart, the building next door is for sale." He didn't need to say which building. He was referring to the ex-brothel, the house that shared a common wall with us. "I'd like to pray about whether or not we're supposed to buy it and turn it into a mission. Lord knows there's enough need."

Then Pat paused and asked the central question. "Suppose the Lord said yes. Would you be willing to stay in Bedford-Stuyvesant?"

I was on the spot. I had said I would be submitting, and right away came this challenge. I did *not* want to raise my children in this place. But on the other hand, with an alive, new part of myself I *did* want to be in the center of God's will.

Slowly, and at a cost which I knew might be immense, I nodded my head.

"Pat," I said, "if this is where the Lord wants us to be, then I'm willing to stay here with you."

What an important moment that turned out to be. It was almost as if the Lord were waiting for Pat and me to be *willing* to yield to Him. Once our hearts were at that point, He began the process of taking us out of Bedford-Stuyvesant altogether.

Event followed event, quickly and to the point. First Pat was sure he heard the Lord tell him to read Jeremiah 16:2. He did not know what the reference would say but opened his Bible and found these incredible words: "Thou shalt not take thee a wife, neither shalt thou have sons or daughters in this place."

We were still rejoicing over that command and still wondering where we *were* supposed to go when something strange happened to me. I was visiting friends from the seminary. Someone asked me, "Dede, do you and Pat know yet what your work is going to be?"

"Yes," I answered, just as quick as that. "The Lord is sending Pat to Virginia to buy a television station."

It was something I just *knew*. There was no explaining it.

When I told Pat about the experience it stimulated again the question of whether or not Christians should become involved in television. So much ugliness spewed out over the airwaves—violence, sex, commercialization that fed man's great greed. How could we consider being part of that?

On the other hand, television was a power tool that the Christian community was not using. "We've allowed this defeat more by default than by being beaten," Pat pointed out.

The Lord was leading us with increasing clarity now. That same night in our bedroom while Pat and I were praying in tongues I thought I heard the Lord urging me to read 1 Chronicles 10:12. I was about to tell Pat when he spoke first.

"Dede," Pat said, "I'm almost certain the Lord is asking me to fast and pray for a week. Is he saying anything to you?"

"Well, yes. I keep hearing the words '1 Chronicles 10:12'."

"Do you know what they say?"

"No I don't, Pat." I was already thumbing through my Bible. These words jumped out at me. ". . . and they fasted seven days."

Twice in succession this mysterious phenomenon had happened to us, and if it never happened again it didn't matter. The Lord was giving us clear, step-by-step directions when we needed them most.

When Pat told Dick Simmons and Dick White of his instructions to go on a fast, they vowed to back him in prayer. The very next morning I helped Pat select a supply of fruit juice. Then I sent him into the adventure of staying in our drafty, dark, old church for seven days.

It was odd not having Pat with us, yet knowing that he was very near. I prayed a lot myself. I asked the Lord to speak clearly to us both.

After the first two days a peace settled over me. The children and I went about our daily routines. When I told them Daddy was next door talking with God, they didn't bat an eye.

At last, the seventh day came and, according to Pat's instructions, I went to the church to get him. Gusts of wind swirled leaves in the entryway as I approached the massive doors. I knocked and heard the sound reverberate inside.

I heard Pat's approaching footsteps. He pulled open the heavy door. The man who stood facing me was radiant! He needed a shave and his hair was mussed and his clothes were rumpled, but there was a set to his shoulders and a light in his eyes that told me more clearly than words that here was a person who had talked with God.

"Dede, I've got the answer," Pat said, a grin suggesting itself around his luminous eyes. "Has He spoken to you, too?"

"Yes," I said, "and I think we have the same message."

"We're going to Virginia," Pat said, standing there holding my hands and grinning at me.

"I know," I said.

We both began to laugh and dance in a circle.

"Come on," he said, his arm around my waist. "Let's go to the altar together and tell Him we accept."

Pat led me through the dark church, lit by one small bulb. We knelt on the dusty, embroidered pad before the altar. The altar's carved wood badly needed polishing; paint was peeling from the high walls of the chancel; grime clouded the stained glass windows. But God was there. In that once-proud church there was a light that came from no man-made source.

"Oh Lord," Pat prayed, "this idea of buying a television station is so crazy. We have no money and no television experience. We're not sure what to do with the station. But we know for sure that You are sending us forth."

I also prayed. "Heavenly Father, we thank You for being so patient with us, for letting us see that Your call is to be a new kind of missionary in a new kind of mission field."

". . . and we look to You, Father," Pat concluded, "to provide all of our needs as well as the money to buy the station."

The rest of the household met us in the parlor. One look at Pat's triumphant face and everyone began to pound him on the back and to congratulate me. Barbara said that she had a word from the Lord for us. "You are going to pioneer a new field," she said, her voice slightly raised. "You will minister as a team and your ministry will one day reach the ends of the earth."

Pat looked startled, but before he had a chance to speak, Dick Simmons called out, "Come on, everybody. Let's celebrate."

With that we trooped down to the kitchen. It looked different to me—less like home and more like someone else's place. The wedding feast at Cana could not have been more joyous. Our wine was juice made from a powder, but we all sat around the oilcloth-covered door-table and sang and praised the Lord.

Over the next few days Pat and I got ready to leave. We were anxious that our parents understand what we were doing, so both of us telephoned home. Pat's father was skeptical, but his mother was delighted. My mother was so glad to see us leave the slums that she wired $100. It was a good thing she did, too, for the U-Haul trailer we had rented for our trip took the very last of our money. We spent $30 of Mother's gift right away for food and gasoline. That left us $70.

"Not much capital is it, Dede!" Pat said, holding out the pitiful handful of bills.

We went to bed that night elated, nonetheless. Both Pat and I felt that we had spent the last two months here in Brooklyn in a preparation time. Perhaps I, more than Pat, needed the preparation. It had been a compressed few weeks, certainly. Four major events happened to me in Brooklyn: I'd agreed to be baptized in water; I had spoken in the language of the Holy Spirit; I'd consented to staying in Brooklyn if that was where God wanted us; and through my submission, Pat and I had become truly one, ready to be used by the Lord in His service.

We arose early that foggy morning in early November to load furniture into the trailer. Harald and Gen called to wish us Godspeed. We stood on the steps of the old brownstone and surveyed our going-away party. There was the Jamaican, towering over everyone even though he stood on the bottom step. The spastic boy and his girl stood together shivering in the autumn chill and waving. Always the leader, Dick Simmons led us in a parting hymn.

We tearfully hugged the team, Alice Blair and Dick White and Dick and Barbara Simmons, and then we joined hands. Pat led us in a prayer of thanksgiving.

How my heart overflowed for the warmth and caring these friends had lavished upon us as we shared our sometimes fiery, always lively hours together in the ghetto.

I wonder if I would have felt quite so warmed had I known that we were to exchange one slum in New York for a different one in Portsmouth. My inventiveness and all of our faith were to be tested as never before in the new life that lay ahead.

JOYOUS BEANS

Half Texas,
half Italian,
we really love
this treat

1½ cups ground, cooked
    soybeans
2 T minced green pepper
2 T minced onion
1 T salad oil
½ cup dry bread crumbs

¼ cup barbecue sauce
1 t salt
1 8 oz. pkg. crescent rolls
4 oz. mozzarella cheese,
    diced
1 egg yolk

    Brown soybeans, green pepper and onion in salad oil.
Remove from heat and add bread crumbs, barbecue sauce
and salt. Set aside. Unroll package of crescent rolls, (which will
become four 8" x 4" rectangles of dough, each of which was
perforated at the factory). Press perforations out of dough
with fingertips. Cut dough in half, yielding eight 4" x 4" pieces.
Place 2 T mixture on each; top with mozzarella cheese. Pull
corners of dough to center, seal with a twist. Beat egg yolk
with 1 t water and brush tops of buns. Bake 15-18 minutes
until golden brown.
    Ground beef may be substituted for part of the beans. This
Texas recipe may be served with hot relishes.

7

JOY

BROOKLYN WAS MANY miles behind us. In a couple of hours we would be crossing Chesapeake Bay on our way into Portsmouth. I'd often heard that the trip across the bay by ferry was an extraordinary experience. I was looking forward to the ride and so were the children. We talked about how the car and trailer would simply drive aboard and be carried across the water.

I remember the joy I felt as we traveled along. It was, in part, the realization that Pat and I were of one mind at last; Pat had made the decision to move to Bedford-Stuyvesant all by himself, but *together* we had made the decision to "claim a television station for the Lord."

It was also, in part, the natural elation of starting a new adventure. This joy came from doing something we had prayed about so thoroughly ahead of time. How could I keep this joy the next time things got tense?

Timmy and Elizabeth were sitting in the back seat of our DeSoto. At seventeen months, Gordon was still in his car seat up front with Pat and me. All of the children traveled well if I stocked the car with plenty of books and played all of the truck-counting games imaginable.

On this particular day when Timmy and Elizabeth grew tired, they settled back in their seats and Tim asked one more time, "Are we almost to the ferry boat, Mommy?"

"When you finish resting, you will open your eyes and see lots of water. And right by the water will be the ferry boat."

Gordon was asleep. Pat was silent. I turned my head to see the two children dozing, snuggled up on the seat like squirrels. Through the back window my eyes once again caught sight of the Boston rocker that had survived the tag sale and was now strapped to the roof of the U-Haul. Beneath that rocker, piled into the orange trailer, were all our earthly possessions from the basement of the manse in Brooklyn. The only thing I had left behind was the lovely English pram Mother had given us. I had passed it on to Barbara for Mary Elizabeth.

Maybe Pat is right, I found myself thinking, my eyes closed. *Maybe the time in Brooklyn* was *meant for me.* Big things had indeed happened in a small space of time. I could remember the anxiety that choked me when we first moved to Brooklyn two months before. It wasn't so much the unsafe neighborhood that filled me with fear; it was the uncertainty. It worried me that Pat had no plan for his life; no job; no ministry on which we were agreed.

And yet, moving to Portsmouth was full of unknowns, too. We had $70 and a scatterbrained idea for buying a television station. Why had I been fear-filled one time and joy-filled now? Was the key that I was taking my eyes off myself long enough to see what He was doing?

One night after supper in the basement kitchen at the manse, all the adults had been sitting around the table praying. It was a time of deep concentration. Most of us were feeling the weight of the oppression of the slums.

"Dear Lord," Dick Simmons had said, "You know how heavy we feel tonight. I lift to You the girl who was stabbed by her brother this morning. And the police officer who was busted for possession. You know how much these people need to know You, Father. Help us . . ."

Just then Tim's bouncing footsteps raced down the stairs.

"Lord," Dick went on, "I lift all of the children in this neighbor . . ."

"Yippee—hey everybody, wanna see something?" Timmy was jumping up and down, his eyes enormous with excitement.

"Hush now, Timmy," Pat said. "Don't you know this is prayer time?"

"But, Dad . . ."

"Go on upstairs, Tim."

"Well, okay," said Timmy, his eyes pleading, "but I can tie a shoe."

"Tie a shoe!" everyone shouted.

"Well now, Pat," said Dick Simmons, "do you think we could take time off to watch Timmy tie a shoe?"

Of course Pat was delighted and agreed. With that Tim very soberly, very methodically, tied his shoe to the wonder of a hushed audience. He looked up waiting for approval and no one disappointed him. Timmy beamed and ran around in a circle. In a minute or two the noise subsided and Timmy happily dashed up to bed.

Well, the entire atmosphere of the prayer time was changed. Where no joy had seemed possible, joy was given us. The time had been heavy, but in the midst of our concerns we were provided with God's light moment. If we let God do the supplying, we could begin to experience joy.

I was determined not to lose this new ground as we

started out on our adventure where so much was bound
to be difficult.

The children woke up just in time to see the big Kipto-
peake Ferry which would take us from Cape Charles
across the bay to the Norfolk-Portsmouth area. We drove
the car and trailer onto the lower deck, then got out.
It was a glorious day. The sun was a yellow mass of fire,
the air chilled in pre-winter freshness. And the waters
of Chesapeake Bay formed whitecaps that blew into foam.
Strange how much more I could see, now that I was free
to enjoy God's world.

Thoughtful George Lauderdale had made arrangements for us to stay for a few days in the home of a
friend, Jean Mayo, a private duty nurse.
. Pat drove the car off the ferry and began to follow
George's direction to Mrs. Mayo's house. I looked out
the car window at the clear sky and remarked to Pat,
"Just hours ago we were driving through streets piled
high with litter. Even the sky in New York was dirty."

Soon we were driving through downtown Portsmouth
and I saw why Pat had made no comment about leaving
littered streets behind. The narrow streets were filled
with trash. Sailors in work fatigues were everywhere.
Newspapers, empty bags and other debris pushed by
gusts of wind from the sea, skittered down the sidewalks.
Still, what I saw were the bright patches of sun and the
intense colors of sky, cloud and water.

At the edge of the downtown area, we stopped for
gas. While Pat called Jean Mayo to tell her that we would
be arriving shortly, I was wondering what our new quarters would be like. We'd be in a "prophet's chamber,"
George had said. I'd never heard the term before. When
I asked Pat what it meant, he said, "Oh, it's a room in
a private home where visiting Christians can stay, like
the upstairs loft the widow kept for Elijah." Somehow

the vision of a prophet's chamber conjured up thoughts
of a suite of rooms in a spacious white mansion. I visual-
ized a staid, proper grande dame greeting us formally
at the door. How was I ever going to explain to this
stranger that we were here to buy a television station
but couldn't even afford a motel room?

A few minutes later we pulled up to a quite simple,
one-story house. An ample, gray-haired, smiling woman
rushed out to greet us. She stooped to hug the children
and was not at all put off when Elizabeth reached up
and patted her braids and wondered aloud how long her
hair was. *"Very* long, Elizabeth. I'll show you, later."

Mrs. Mayo led the way to our new quarters—a tiny
back room about ten by twelve feet. Timmy and Elizabeth would sleep on Mrs. Mayo's sofa. I smiled at the
thought of our progress: it seemed we were forever moving to smaller quarters. First there was my parents' home
in Ohio, then our four-room apartment in Queens, then
our one-and-a-half rooms in Brooklyn. And now, this tiny
place.

Well, small room or not, I couldn't help but marvel
at this unusual woman who was willing to take in five
people for who knows how long! Mrs. Mayo helped me
give the children a light supper, bathe them and put
them to bed. Afterwards she fixed us all a snack and we
sat talking. To my surprise Mrs. Mayo was not abashed
at the thought of buying a TV station when we had no
money. "God is good at making something out of nothing," she said. "You can be sure that if you're doing His
will, He will do the supplying."

It was obvious to me that with this prophet's chamber
in her smallish home Mrs. Mayo was practicing what she
preached. She turned over to the Lord the little she had
and then let Him make what He wanted out of it. Would
it work for us too?

The following morning Pat called George Lauderdale
and told him we were going to drive out to the station
to look around. When he hung up he turned to Mrs. Mayo.
"George said to be prepared. Apparently Spratley Street
is not exactly in the most glamorous neighborhood?"

Mrs. Mayo smiled. *"That* I'd agree to. But remember,
God can build out of nothing."

The children were content to stay with Mrs. Mayo,
so we unhitched the trailer which we had rented for
two weeks so we could have a place for storing our things,
then headed toward Spratley Street. I leaned back,
tingling with excitement. We were actually going to see
our TV station. I was imagining something out of Holly-
wood. I could hardly wait until we got there to see what
God was about to give us.

But as we drove, I noticed that the closer we got to
the water the shabbier the houses became. We passed
through an especially depressed section of two-story, un-
painted, rundown, frame homes. We asked one young
boy for directions to the station and found we were just
a few blocks away.

Pat and I were silent as we drove on. Spratley Street
ran next to a body of water called Scott's Creek. It wasn't
the kind of quick-running creek I was used to in Ohio.
This was a tidal area, and when the tide was out, as it
was now, debris stuck up out of the ooze.

"Where do you think the station is, Honey?" I asked
Pat, sniffing at the fishy smell.

There was something up ahead that *might* be a trans-
mitting tower. It had loose wires hanging from it, but
there were no studios except for a brick and masonry
building sitting on a rubble-filled lot amidst blown November weeds.

Since there were no other possibilities, Pat drove into
what could have been called a parking area in front of

the building. We just sat there and looked. Vandals had
broken the windows. The front door had been forced.
Something that looked like film was strewn about.

"Well, come on, Dede. There's no point sitting here.
Let's go visit our studio."

We walked up to the building and looked in. It was
total wreckage. The studio was easy to walk into, and
we did. Glass and papers were underfoot everywhere. I
had never seen Pat so discouraged. He walked around
kicking at the debris, and then he stood in the middle
of the mess, hands on his hips and stared, stoop-shoul-
dered, not saying one word.

"All I can say is that God *has* to be in this if it's ever
going to be turned into something useful," Pat said finally.
He turned and looked around once more, then walked
into the control room. Instruments lay strewn amid overturned chairs. Shaking his head fast, as though trying
to rid himself of some overwhelming thought, he said,
"Come on, Dede. Let's go."

As we drove back down Spratley Street I kept feeling
a nudge to say something. I even knew *what* I was supposed to say. But each time I opened my mouth, I'd have
second thoughts. So I kept silent until at last the urging
became so strong that I knew I just had to tell Pat what,
perhaps, the Lord was saying to me.

"Pat, back at the station God told me we are operating
under a commission. Making something out of nothing
is His responsibility, not ours. All we have to do is watch
Him at work and walk through the tasks He gives us to
do."

Pat listened in silence, but there was a quiet, almost-
smile on his lips. He and I both knew that these were
strange words from me, not at all the kind I was accustomed to uttering. I found that they filled me with a
special reassurance, and I wondered if by any chance

they were a kind of prophecy. Uttering them in obedience brought me joy too. Obedience meant getting out of His way so He could act, and that produced joy.

At Mrs. Mayo's house, Pat called Harald and Gen collect, apologizing to them for doing so, but saying he'd settle up later. He wanted to tell them about the station. While he talked I described to Mrs. Mayo what a complete shambles the place was.

"If it is in such poor condition," Mrs. Mayo said, "perhaps they won't ask much for it. In the meantime, why don't you visualize the station God is even now creating."

But it wasn't only the television station the Lord would have to create out of nothing. There was the matter of our finding an apartment with our cash supply down now to about $40. How was the Lord going to solve that problem? One morning in prayer Pat heard the word "boulevard." So we began looking at apartments on boulevards. At an intersection of two boulevards was a duplex brick apartment house that appeared, from the number of naval station stickers on the cars in the parking lot, to be used primarily by navy people. Pat parked and we walked into Stanley Court which overlooked a large open field. The manager showed us the one apartment that was available. The downstairs had a living room, dining area and kitchen and the upstairs had three bedrooms!

I held my breath as Pat talked finances. "We can't give you any rent money in advance, and we don't have enough for a security deposit either . . ."

There was a long silence. The manager looked intently at Pat, and then abruptly handed us the keys. "I pride myself on knowing an honest face," he said. We'd just witnessed a homey, caring miracle.

We drove back to Mrs. Mayo's house as excited as children. The very next day we thanked her for having given us so much, hugged her good-by, and made our way to the apartment.

It was quite an experience unpacking our U-Haul. The pathetic few pieces of furniture were lost in the apartment. The three upstairs rooms had almost nothing in them. Pat and I had bought a new mattress and springs, but we had no bedstead. The only frills were the unbleached muslin drapes I'd made in Queens, and our pair of silver candelabra. Thanksgiving came just a few days after we moved into our new, spacious, but thinly appointed quarters. We wanted to express our appreciation to George Lauderdale and his wife and invited them to have dinner with us. What a unique Thanksgiving that was. We bought a turkey and ate by candlelight in the grand tradition . . . but our "table" was an old moving trunk, and except for the one Boston rocker, our "chairs" were either the floor or the steps.

Early the next week Pat tried to reach the owner of the abandoned television station, Tim Bright, but he lived in Baltimore, and no one seemed to know where he was. We drove out to the station again and were just as discouraged as before, which perhaps explains the timing of a pleasant surprise. The Lord began His process of supplying our practical, everyday needs by bringing to our landlord's attention the fact that we were sleeping on a mattress on the floor. He told us that many of the people at Stanley Court were transients so he occasionally rented furniture. For $10 a month!

"I can show you what I have on hand," he offered. Pat went with him and was amazed to see a colonial living room suite similar to the one Pat had sold. The manager also had a dining room set, a round, expandable, pine table with captain's chairs to match. By the time we finalized our agreement we had a fully furnished house, and now all we had to do was find some way to earn the $10 a month that it cost us.

Which brought Pat and me once again to the question of my working. It wasn't always easy for me to live in the new submitted role, especially when Pat's decisions just didn't make sense. Here we were barely scraping by. Pat couldn't take a regular job; he felt that trying to purchase the TV station *was* his work. Occasionally an opportunity opened up to preach, but he wasn't always paid. Our folks helped out occasionally with a little money or a ham or a turkey. But in the meantime the expenses of living went right on.

So, in spite of the fact that he didn't like the idea, Pat agreed that I should look for work. I walked to nearby Portsmouth General Hospital and applied for a job. The hospital was shorthanded and once again, as I had in Queens, I just walked right into a job. I couldn't wait to go to work. Elizabeth pretended to be pressing her doll's dress next to me as I ironed my white uniform. Then at three o'clock Friday afternoon I kissed Pat and the children good-by and headed for Portsmouth General. What a wonderful experience this was going to be, as a Christian nurse. Now I would be able to minister to more than just the physical man; now I could help the whole person.

But from Pat's point of view the arrangement was a disaster. My job was on weekends—Friday, Saturday, and Sunday. It often worked out that my relief didn't show up on time. On other days there was a crisis at the hospital, and I just couldn't leave my patients. So I often worked late. I'd arrive home exhausted only to face a disoriented family. They felt I was away longer than I really was. After my demanding weekend it took until Tuesday to feel like a human being again. On Wednesday I started getting ready for the following weekend. So the three-day job turned out to be full time as far as the family was concerned.

Once again soybeans were on our table. I had to be continually inventive. Here in Tidewater we either ate soybeans or we didn't eat. Whenever the children, especially Tim, complained about the monotony of our diet, Pat told him gently that he should not murmur, because this food was like the manna of the Bible—it was all there *was*.

But I could understand Tim's point. I did everything possible to make our "Tribulation food" different and attractive. Whenever I could scrape up enough dimes I bought the extras that turn soybean meals into delicacies. I had a recipe for "Joyous Beans" which was a real celebration meal: crescent rolls surrounding hamburger, ground soybeans and mozzarrella cheese. That dish looked like something from a magazine. And I also continued to serve my "Love Waffles" with homemade jam, and my "Peace Button Cookies" which were spiced with ginger and cinnamon and pecans. Even when we did manage to put a little ground beef on the table it was always with soybean mash as a meat extender. The children never knew the difference. So despite the hardship, we had plenty of food on the table—good food too.

I continued to be surprised by the joy I felt throughout these difficult days. The joy came from the new side of my life, where instead of *fretting* I was *watching*—watching Him provide.

One day, for instance, while Pat was trying once again to get together with Tim Bright for the purchase of the station, there was a knock at the front door. Timmy ran to answer and there stood half a dozen strangers, all men. They were holding large cardboard cartons.

"Is this the Robertsons'?"

"Yes, Sir," said Timmy as I came up behind him. The men filed into the apartment and put their heavy boxes down on our rented pine table in the dining room and introduced themselves. They came from the church where Pat had preached a few weeks earlier in December. Pat had mentioned that we were eating soybeans. Apparently the thought was so unusual that the church decided to take steps.

"This is a 'pounding,' Mrs. Robertson," the minister said as he and the deacons unloaded the canned goods, flour, Jello, fresh vegetables, cereals.

"A *pounding*?"

"Yes, Ma'am. We have a tradition here. When someone needs food, each person in the church supplies a pound of this and a pound of that—which makes a pounding."

The children were delighted and started examining the cookies and soft drinks. I watched in amazement, wondering if my kitchen cupboards could even hold such bounty. The children went from box to box taking out things and shouting, "Hey look—cereal! Mom, can we try some, can we?"

Our visitors were as pleased as we were. We all sat down for tea and cookies and discussed God's ways of providing, which soon turned into a discussion of the television station. It was going to be a joy, I said, watching God provide there too. He would use many avenues of provision: the church, natural means, mystical means.

But why is it that having started to learn to depend upon Him, we tend to go on doing things our way? Despite the blessings from the Lord, the midwinter months were difficult for us. Something was wrong. Pat was doing far too much running again. He was speaking at churches and at Rotary Clubs or wherever people would listen to his dream of a Christian broadcasting station.

This whole story of the founding of CBN is told in detail in Pat's book and I won't cover it again here except to say that once more Pat was coming home at all hours. I knew he was under strain from the way he collapsed into bed at night. And I was under strain, too, from the taxing hours at the hospital.

Then one windy, chilly day Tim wanted to assemble a kite we had given him. As Elizabeth and Gordon watched, Tim and I sat on the living room floor with balsa wood strips and sheets of red and yellow tissue paper spread out on the brown, oval, braided rug. When the kite was finished, I wrapped Tim snugly in sweater and jacket, all the while urging him not to be in too big a hurry.

"You know, Tim, kite flying takes a lot of room. I really think we ought to wait until I can take you to the park."

"No, I want to try it now. Don't worry, I'll be careful."

So I let him go.

Timmy headed outdoors and I went into the kitchen to watch him. He put the kite on the ground, held the string and ran as fast as he could. The kite dragged along the ground and rose a few inches, then plummeted. Tim then held the string closer to the kite and tried again. This time he managed to get it to fly a little higher. On his third try, he met with success. A wind lifted the kite, until it swayed and seesawed in the blue sky.

Timmy held his head back, his red hair blowing in the wind. I'm sure he was saying to himself, "You see, Mom, I did it."

But at this moment the branch of a tree caught the kite's string. The tree slashed into the kite's frail tissue.

Oh, Timmy, why couldn't you wait? I said, half out loud.

Tim's hand let go of the string. His shoulders sagged. He put his hands in his pockets and walked slowly towards home.

I opened the door. Without raising his head, Tim brushed past me mumbling, "I know you're going to say 'I told you so.'"

"Then I won't say it, Tim." I knelt down next to him and held him in my arms. I felt his ribs shudder in his effort to keep from crying. "All of us are impatient sometimes." Even as I spoke I knew I was talking to myself and to Pat. "Mommy and Daddy, too. We sometimes just don't wait for God's timing."

So a very pensive little boy shuffled off to his room. As I watched him I realized how like us our son had been that morning. Proud and headstrong, Pat and I were bound and determined to do things ourselves. We couldn't wait for the Lord. In our work we were running ahead of His timing for us.

When I told Pat the parable of the kite that night, we both chuckled. Surely the Lord was speaking to all of us at once—Tim, Pat and me.

The very next day we began to pray together, whenever we could do so, for the courage to wait for God's timing. We did far less worrying. Instead, our energy went into expecting. As we did so, sure enough, negotiations began to fall into place:

• The Lord had given Pat the figure of $37,000 as the price he was to pay for the television station, free of all debts and encumbrances. The station was worth perhaps 10 times that much. Yet on January 3, 1960 Pat made this offer to Tim Bright.

• Since we did not have anything close to $37,000, Pat secured from Tim Bright a six-month option on the station at "God's price."

• On January 11, 1960 the nonprofit corporation charter for the Christian Broadcasting Network was filed with the State of Virginia. The board of directors consisted of Pat and me, George Lauderdale, Harald Bredesen and Bob Walker.

PEACE BUTTONS

Great TV snack, unless you're dieting!

1 cup corn oil margarine
1½ cups brown sugar
1 egg
½ cup soybeans, cooked and ground
2 cups unbleached flour
1 t baking soda
½ t salt
1 t cinnamon
1 t ginger
1 t vanilla
1 cup chopped pecans
powdered sugar

Cream margarine, add brown sugar and egg and beat well. Add cooked, ground soybeans, then flour, baking soda, salt, cinnamon, ginger and mix well. Fold in the pecans and vanilla. Chill mixture for several hours. Form the dough into one-inch balls, and roll them in the powdered sugar. Place on cookie sheet and bake at 375° for 10 to 12 minutes. Yields approximately 24 Peace Buttons.

PEACE

SPRING COMES EARLY to the Tidewater region of Virginia, so we were already into summerish weather in May of 1960 when I sensed that the Lord was bringing us into a new, more difficult phase of His teaching process.

Pat and I liked to take evening walks with the children, just before sunset. After six months in the apartment, we all were becoming familiar with the neighborhood surrounding our home. With the negotiations for the television station finally resolved, I should have been at peace. But something undefined and illusive was gnawing at me.

The unrest would surface on our walks. Several blocks from the apartment was a vacant, two-story, white shingle farmhouse which belonged to a church where we often worshiped. The farmhouse captured my heart, but for the life of me I really couldn't tell why. To all appearances it was just a crummy old building. But there were flowering crabapple and mulberry trees in the yard and at one time there had been a garden, although now the place was buried in a wilderness of weeds.

125

That's not what I saw, however. I imagined the yard as it could be, all cleaned up. My yearning for that house became a joke between Pat and me. He would catch me eyeing my farmhouse and wag a finger. " 'Thou shalt not covet thy neighbor's house.' Exodus 20:17," he'd quote with a grin.

This home, neglected though it was, pointed to something sorely missing from our lives—settledness! New Haven, Staten Island, Queens, Brooklyn, Mrs. Mayo's home, the Stanley Court apartment; we were always transients. How I yearned for a place we could really call home.

And then a few months later an unexpected thing happened! Pat was offered the farmhouse! The church made it clear that they would have to reclaim the house as soon as they could build a new church. But we could live there in the meantime.

I was ecstatic. Even the new address was music to me: we would be living on Deep Creek Boulevard. It was a thrill to be handed the keys by a deacon's wife, just before we were to move in, so that we could decide where we wanted to put our furniture.

Our furniture? Then I realized she didn't know that we had none of our own but had rented furniture with the apartment.

Still, key in hand we walked down to the farmhouse. The children and I enjoyed planning where the furniture that we didn't have might go in the house we could never own. Elizabeth and Timmy raced up the front steps with Gordon tottering after them. Then they ran up and down the length of the front porch, turning it into an imaginary battleship at Tim's urging.

The front door entered into the gray-painted, plank-floored living room. Beyond it was the dining room with the kitchen off of that. The furnace was in the kitchen, a gray octopus whose tentacles conducted heat by way of exposed pipes throughout the dwelling. As I was puzzling over how to disguise the monstrosity, Timmy shouted, "Wow, Mom, our ship's even got a boiler room!" And I knew this crew would never let me conceal such a vital plaything so long as we lived there.

I heard the children stomping around upstairs where they discovered another unique feature: an old-fashioned, high-sided bathtub that stood on claw-shaped feet. All three children climbed in with cries of "Man the lifeboats! Man the lifeboats!" They weren't the least concerned that our new home had no furniture. Who needs furniture when there's already a lifeboat on the battleship?

We got permission from the church to repaint the floors of the old farmhouse, turning them from gray to a Williamsburg green. As soon as the paint was dry, friends from the church came over to help us move. When they discovered that we would again be using the old trunk as a dining room table, they loaned us a picnic table. I laughed to myself. All I had to do was cover it with oilcloth and we'd be back in the kitchen at the manse in Brooklyn.

Fortunately, my unbleached muslin curtains fit the windows in the new house. And our round braided rug accented the Williamsburg green floors. The Boston rocker and Pat's trunk and the picnic table comprised our furniture on the first floor. We added to this with purchases made from the Union Mission and from regular visits to garage sales. But the nicest gifts of all came from my mother who volunteered to send us some of the family's spare furniture. When it arrived it was almost too good to be true. Moving men trooped in and within minutes our farmhouse was turned into my own place complete with a couch and a wingback chair.

I breathed a prayer: "Oh Lord, thank You for Your provision through Mother. *We* may be temporary, but there's nothing temporary about *You!*"

We lived in this home for two years, from the late summer of 1960 to the summer of 1962, far longer than we'd expected. As I anticipated I especially liked the house for its garden. I spent hours there. As soon as Timmy was off to school at eight-thirty in the morning I headed for the yard. Elizabeth played happily with a bucket and toy shovel, Gordon explored every cranny of the yard, and I worked to rescue the remnants of an earlier garden from the honeysuckle.

Still, I was uncomfortable.

What is there about the Holy Spirit that gives one such a sixth sense? Even though we were thoroughly settled on Deep Creek Boulevard I knew that we were being prepared for harder times ahead. This was just an interlude, a rest period before an entirely different kind of life came into focus. It was a time of encouragement, preparing us for what lay ahead.

For Pat, encouragement was needed as he tried to get the broadcast ministry accepted. He was criticized even before he got off the ground. Several pastors began to regard him as unsound just because he was working in television.

My own concern was our inability to settle down. Perhaps this is always a larger issue for women than for men. We resist a temporary life style based on minute-by-minute supply. But perhaps this is the way God always provides for us . . . temporarily. Even when we think we are settled, we never know when we'll be *un*settled. I remembered Pat's teaching on the Old Testament concept of the sojourner. God, Pat pointed out, had a special love for the sojourner who was always being uprooted.

Why was I suddenly remembering that dream of mine from college days? Does God know we are all about to become sojourners again and thus is vitally interested in communicating to us just how He will provide for us during hard times?

In the summer of 1962 we left our farmhouse and its now beautiful garden. But God did not leave us untended even for a few days. This time He used a local philanthropist, Fred Beasley, as His instrument. Mr. Beasley offered Pat two things: first, he provided Pat with a gift of $100 each week so that he could work full time at the television station; and second, he offered us a rent-free house that belonged to the Beasley Foundation.

I was delighted and thankful, but I'm afraid I was also unsettled when I heard the address. The house was on "B" Street, just a stone's throw from the studio. So I knew ahead of time that it was situated in the heart of a far-less-than-glamorous neighborhood!

Nonetheless Pat and I and the children piled into the car and went to check out our possible new home. Most of the houses were single-story frame, with yards in the front and in back. The best-kept features were the fences, which seemed to say, "Keep out."

We finally found the house on a dead-end street, parked the car and surveyed the building. At least it was freshly painted and attractive in contrast to the neglected houses we'd been passing. On one side was a Boy Scout center, and across the street was a community swimming pool. Out back was a small, overgrown yard. Beyond the back fence appropriately enough, it seemed to me, was a graveyard.

"It's not the best location, Sweetheart," Pat said. "But the children can use the playground. And there won't be any through traffic."

Pat opened the car door for the kids who darted out
to survey the premises. Why aren't they seeing this place
as a disaster! The ground was hardpan, just like the Brooklyn yard had been. I could never grow a garden here!
"Pat . . . " I mumbled.

Pat turned and faced me. There was no guile in his
voice as he said, "Dede, I know how you feel." There
was a long silence. "But if it's God's place for us He'll
make it all right."

There was nothing more to say. I knew I should feel
thankful for a free home, but all I did feel was guilt at
my *lack* of thankfulness. We returned to our house on
Deep Creek Boulevard and began assembling our belongings for the move to "B."

To complicate matters I discovered that I was expecting again. The new pregnancy left me emotionally
drained at times. The longer we lived on "B" Street the
more I appreciated the house and the less I appreciated
the setting. The building was more attractive and would
be easier to decorate than the Deep Creek place, although there were open cracks in the floor. I missed my
garden though, and I just didn't have the energy to start
all over again in that bad soil.

On "B" Street I had the impression that some alien
force was working against the neighborhood. It was as
if the people had given up hope. I felt mistrust in the
eyes of the preteens who hung around the Boy Scout
center, and in the mothers who brought their children
to the community pool across the way. One neighbor
was very brusque with me. Her husband seemed to be
away most of the time, and she was carrying on a turbulent love affair with his cousin.

But even in the midst of these days God was preparing
an escape from the depression that was settling over me.

In those days CBN was starting to establish a sound financial reputation, which pleased Pat very much. But Pat, being Pat, only saw this as an opportunity to *give* more. At almost exactly the time Pat succeeded in securing a $12,000 loan, he also received a letter from an old friend.

"Do you remember Dove Toll, Dede?" Pat asked me over his tea one morning in our "B" Street kitchen. He held an envelope in his hand, with a strange, oriental-looking stamp on it. Yes, I remembered Dove Toll. She was our friend from seminary prayer-group days. She was the young woman with the special dream of sending Korean Christians out as missionaries.

"Well," Pat went on, "Dove is in Korea, just as she hoped, and . . . " Pat held up the letter. " . . . she is sticking with her vision. In fact she's asking CBN for $1,000 to send a Korean Christian named Mrs. Lea to Bolivia as a missionary . . . "

I was interested but only distantly. We certainly couldn't think of sending anyone $1,000. Pat had just borrowed the money himself!

" . . . so I was thinking," Pat's eyes were alive, sparkling in that special way of his, when he seems to be sensing God's own delight, " . . . I was thinking maybe we could use a thousand of that loan and send it to Dove for her 'Mrs. Lea'."

I suppose it would have been possible for me to argue with Pat, trying to bring a little sense to his logic. Should we give money away when we ourselves were borrowing? But I knew the kind of answer Pat would give me: If God had brought us to a strong enough position to take out a loan, then we should be willing to help other parts of the Christian body of believers who were in need.

It didn't make sense to me, but I didn't argue because there were other areas in our lives far more volatile. We were, in fact, living through one of the worst periods in our marriage. The new baby wasn't due until April 1963, but a month before that I knew I was headed for trouble. Part of the problem was physical. March in the Tidewater area of Virginia can be blisteringly cold and windy. We spent a fortune on oil but couldn't seem to heat the house more than a few degrees above the temperature out of doors. Wind and cold blasted through the cracks in the floor.

As hard as the physical conditions were, it was an older problem that really hurt. Pat was doing more than any one man should attempt. Trying to run the television stations was a double full-time job all by itself, but on top of that Pat was standing in at WXRI, a radio station we had acquired. It all added up to a repetition of the very early days of our marriage. On many occasions Pat worked 20 hours a day. Of course I felt sorry for him. But I also felt left out. The four hours a day that were left over weren't exactly prime time.

And then, just before the baby was due, measles struck our family. Elizabeth was the first to get sick. A few days later Gordon came down too. In the midst of this I had to pack my suitcase and make arrangements to be admitted to the hospital. At four o'clock in the morning, April 24, 1963, I awoke with the familiar contractions. Ann was born just an hour later, healthy and hungry.

But the world she came into was not an easy one for Pat and me. Pat still couldn't find anyone to take his shift at the radio station which meant that his visits to the hospital during my five-day stay were practically nonexistent. When he did come it was with bad news. Elizabeth was better, but Gordon was one mighty sick little boy. When Pat was home he had to be both mother and father again to the children. He was, I knew, a good father whenever possible, reading to the children and playing the happy roughhouse games he was so good at. But I also knew that those times with Tim and Elizabeth and Gordon just didn't come very often.

When Ann and I finally came home, a post-partum depression took control of my spirits. The trouble was partly physical, a common problem for many women after childbirth. It was also a reaction to my worry over Gordon who needed almost constant nursing in his recovery. Add all these emotions together, shake them in with a brand new baby and two older children who needed extra attention and. . . .

It was in the middle of this mayhem that the Lord stepped in.

To this day I really don't understand how He did it. Some of His provision for me had been obvious, but this time He was very subtle. All I can say is that I met a Spirit-baptized couple in Columbus and that they were able to pass their own peace on to me; I have no idea how the mystery was performed. Perhaps that is the nature of any miracle.

It all began routinely enough. The children and I drove out to Columbus for a traditional long holiday around the Fourth of July. It was so great to take 10-week-old Ann into the rooms of my childhood home and whisper to her about the happy events that had taken place there. One thing I did not share even with my infant daughter was that strange, still-alive dream which had occurred right in this same house when I was in college. The memory supplied me with a flick of excitement, for the dream was beginning to come to pass. The man now existed, and so did the other people who "belonged" to me: They were my children.

But it was still not an experience I could talk about, certainly not with my parents. Mother might possibly understand; she continued to read her Bible in her own

reserved and private way. But Dad would never hear
me out; he was still his practical, always-cheerful self,
and his response to the dream would not have changed
over the years.

So, as I had always done, I kept my own counsel.

Sunday came. Pat had told me that there was a very
alive church in Columbus, the Broad Street United Methodist. So I went. After the service I introduced myself
to the pastor and his wife, a pleasant couple, David and
Nina Skeen. Almost immediately I sensed that David and
Nina were Godsent. Their warmth and peace were mixed
with a contagious enthusiasm, and I knew right away
that I wanted to see more of them.

"Where are you staying?" David asked. When I gave
him my folks' address he was delighted. "Why that's just
two blocks away from our home, so of course you'll come
for a visit."

What is more special than God's gift of just-the-right-
people-at-just-the-right-time? I wonder if the Skeens even
knew how much they meant to me during the month
that I stayed in Columbus. It wasn't so much what they
said as what they *were* that helped me. Every time I
went to their home or to their church I knew that God's
joy was alive and well. His peace was available to His
people, including me. I remember one evening in particular when the Skeens invited me to the weekly Bible
study they held in their home. What a fragile, beautiful
evening. Nothing special happened. No grand emotion,
no great, resounding message. It was mostly a night of
praise. I sat on a high-backed sofa, relaxed and just drank
in the Spirit. I came away so refreshed that I *knew* I
had turned a corner.

And indeed I had. When I got back to Virginia I discovered that not only was I refreshed and ready to meet
life on "B" Street, but Pat, too, had experienced a time

of recovery. At first when we talked about it we put the change down to pressure being eased, but later we realized that what had happened to us was far more mystic than that! God had given us both the gift of His peace when we needed it most.

Almost exactly a year later I found myself thinking how happy we were now. I had spent a year rejoicing. Not all the time, of course, but as a steady diet nonetheless. We were all well. Our parents were well. Pat and I loved each other. In spite of the way we teased each other at times, we had an on-going romance in our lives. We were two sometimes rather difficult people God had put together to grow up in Him side by side. We were a true team again, both supporting each other in the ministry of CBN. We still ate soybeans (although now it was only very occasionally) but most of the time there was enough steady income to put meat on the table.

What this victory amounted to—what the Lord had been teaching me—was that His peace is independent of a *place*. We were still on "B" Street, and I was still uncomfortable there.

But I was at peace.

The encouragement continued. God began to show us how far ahead-of-the-event He is preparing His different kinds of supply.

One day Pat came home all excited. "Dede," he said, putting a letter down on the kitchen table, "you'll never guess what's been happening over the past several years without our ever knowing it. Do you remember Dove Toll's Korean friend, Mrs. Lea? The one Dove sent to Bolivia?"

I nodded, remembering that CBN had helped financially. There was that light in Pat's eyes which comes when he catches a glimpse of the hidden ways of God.

"Well," Pat said, picking up the letter and tapping it lightly, "Dove wrote back that several years ago this same Mrs. Lea was invited by a retired Methodist missionary to visit the States. While Mrs. Lea was here, she and her Methodist missionary friend spent a lot of time praying for . . . guess what?"

I raised my eyebrows in answer.

"They prayed for a Christian *television* station here in Norfolk!"

"Really, Pat? How remarkable."

"And they kept praying—for years. So it's full circle. Now, the very Christian TV station they prayed for is sending Mrs. Lea to Bolivia. That's the way God's economy works."

And the children! They were a series of four absolutely different delights. Ann was a year-old toddler now and an incredible child in that she was an escape artist. I would be cooking something in the sparsely-equipped kitchen and turn my head for just one minute. When I looked up there was our little explorer, stumping down "B" Street, determinedly heading in the direction of downtown Portsmouth. Once, while it was unusually cool weather in the late spring of 1964, I looked up at the flash of something in our front yard. It was the bare derriere of Ann, streaking away. As I burst through the front door in pursuit, I nearly tripped in her diapers on the front stoop.

One evening at dusk I looked out the back to see Gordon and some neighborhood boys playing hide-and-seek among the tombstones. Here was Gordon enjoying himself, completely free from the anxiety older kids might feel at frolicking about among people's graves.

For her part, Elizabeth adapted to "B" Street in a totally different way. She was almost eight and was attending school in the neighborhood where she really enjoyed making friends. More than once she would elegantly invite a young girl friend home after school for "tea." Elizabeth, it seemed, told all her friends that I made the best oatmeal and praline cookies in all of Portsmouth.

And Timmy was learning to cope in a far tougher world than the one in which Pat and I had been raised. Tim liked "B" Street. He also liked his fourth-grade teacher who got him interested in learning, and he liked playing rough and tumble ball across the way. Timmy held his own quite well with the neighborhood boys, even when they turned on him, as happened one hot evening.

Pat and I sat in the house with all the windows open, trying to catch a cooling breeze. Suddenly, we heard a terrible ruckus outside. The children were screaming and Elizabeth crashed through the screen door to tell us Tim needed help, fast! We rushed out in time to see a gang of boys banging Timmy against a concrete wall at the center.

Pat roared them off, and we walked Tim back to our house.

"I really don't know what happened," Tim said as he wiped tears from his cheeks. "All of a sudden they just jumped me."

I told him it would never happen again.

"But how do you know, Mom?"

"Because Dad and I are going to ask the Lord to protect you, that's how."

But this experience put a new light on "B" Street. For all their adaptability, the children were in danger from time to time, and Pat and I just couldn't protect all four of them, nor did we think we should try.

A schoolboy fight was one thing, but possible arson was another.

It was early on a summer morning. The children were

playing around the house, Pat was at the studio, and I was making the beds. I heard the voices of some children in the backyard. "Odd," I said to myself. "I don't recognize those voices." I looked out the window but didn't see anyone. So I turned back to my work.

But a few minutes later I smelled something burning outside and heard a crackling sound. I looked out to see smoke coming from the storage lean-to that was attached to the house.

As calmly as I could, I hustled everyone out of the house, then I called the fire department. It wasn't until the children heard the screaming sirens that they realized our shed was ablaze!

I was scared because there was little way in which that shed could have caught fire by natural means. It was not wired for electricity and was only used for dry storage. Our clothes were there in the big trunk, the kids' bicycles were there, and some demitasse cups I had collected, plus a relic of my childhood—a precious nativity scene which I'd taken out every Christmas since the year after I learned there was no Santa Claus!

The firemen worked quickly. As one hosed down the building, two others went inside and began salvaging our belongings. They tossed out Timmy's and Elizabeth's bicycles, then our clothes from the trunk, all in a heap. Finally, with the same swift efficiency, they threw out the boxes containing the demitasse cups and the nativity scene. Many of the demitasse cups were ruined, but the nativity scene miraculously was intact. Just a little scorched!

A neighbor called Pat. He rushed over from the studio just as the firemen were leaving. Pat and I were sobered by the fire because we strongly suspected arson. What if it had been our house instead of just the shed? Was there someone who disliked us enough to set fire to our house the next time?

"Come on," Pat said, "let's ask the Lord right now to show us what we should do."

Pat and I knelt together beside the couch Mother had sent us.

"Heavenly Father," Pat began, "we thank You for all Your provisions since we arrived here in Portsmouth. But Lord, Dede and I are not sure we should go on living in this house. Lord, we probably can endure more, but we ask You now to supply us with a new place to live just as soon as possible."

"Amen!" I added.

Pat and I arose from our knees. We knew that our testing time, the time when we learned how to have peace in the midst of insecurity, was coming to an end.

FAITH HAMBURGERS

Some people prefer this dish to the all-beef variety

2 cups ground cooked
  soybeans
¼ cup chopped parsley
1 t salt
¼ t pepper

2 egg yolks, beaten
2 T evaporated milk or
  cream

Mix together and shape into patties. Dip in flour and chill for 1 hour. Sauté slowly in butter or fat and serve with barbecue sauce or catsup.

You may substitute ½ cup ground beef for equivalent amount of soybeans if desired, for more meat flavor. Serves four.

9

FAITH

THE LORD HAD specifically warned us, I felt, that we were to leave "B" Street. But Pat, though equally ready to move, wanted to be sure we acted only when we moved in faith not in fear.

"How will we know when that is, Daddy?" Tim asked one hot Sunday morning when we were having a rare sit-down breakfast with every member of the family present. Pat looked at me with a slight smile, and I just knew what he was thinking, that these were the ideal times for training children—when *they* asked questions.

So that morning Pat explained in boy-terms that faith itself was a gift from God, but that especially at turning-point times in life you just didn't dare make a move without it. So you asked for the gift of faith in the particular situation you faced.

And that's what we did. As a family we asked God to give us the faith to hear Him about our move. Maybe we'd hear in our hearts, Pat said, or maybe the Lord would speak through the Bible or through circumstances. We'd see.

As it turned out God spoke through circumstances.

Mr. Beasley offered us another rent-free house!

And through that house I came into a confrontation with that old "Secret Dream" that had been sitting quietly, unfadingly, in my memory since college days.

One evening in August 1964, Pat came home smiling. I could see that he had good news.

"Dede, you're not going to believe this. Do you remember that big old house Mr. Beasley's foundation owns out on the grounds of Frederick College?" I did indeed remember the house—a white, frame building with four square columns across the front. "We can move in right away," Pat said.

The next day all six of us piled into the car and drove out to the flat farmland that skirted the brackish tidal waters on the edge of Norfolk. We turned off the blacktop highway, drove past the gatekeeper's cottage at Frederick College, wound our way over a smaller road through a woods until at last we rounded a bend, and there was the house.

A driveway led through an avenue of trees. We just sat in the car for a moment, looking. The pillared colonial was bracketed by two huge, gracious, twin magnolia trees. Out back I could just see the waterway that traced its path through the marsh. The place was very, very quiet except for the birds. There were birds everywhere: cardinals and mockingbirds and crows and ducks and purple grackle and even a heron.

"Was this a plantation with slaves and things?" Elizabeth asked.

"It was a truck farm," Pat told her. "Barges used to tie up there in back, where they were loaded with produce for the city."

Then—quite unexpectedly—while Pat and the children got out of the car I began to experience an eerie sensation. A chill ran up my spine. *Could this be the country house of my dream?* There it was, the large house, the marsh that could be interpreted as a lake, the pine trees.

I just couldn't wait to see if there was a cellar.

I got slowly out of the car and followed Pat toward the house with a feeling almost of predestination, as if I were supposed to be here. But since I couldn't explain what was happening, I said nothing. Pat's conversation, so practical, so everyday, offset my own excitement as we walked around.

Pat's reaction was predictably enthusiastic. "Just think what a touch of paper and paint would do to this place, Dede."

"It looks haunted," Tim said gloomily.

Pat unlocked the door. We stepped in. The house had been unoccupied for years. There in the dusky interior we found ourselves in an entry hall. Before us was a winding staircase leading to the second floor. To the right was the dining room which would be sunny and cheerful, I thought, if the house were properly opened. We turned to the left into the living room and then into a den behind it and on to a veranda at the back of the house. We walked upstairs where there were four bedrooms, small-ish but flooded with sunlight.

But, I noticed with a little puzzlement, there was no basement entrance to be found anywhere. Off the kitchen there was a small catch-all room where the house's oil furnace sat in a small well, slightly below the level of the floor, but that was certainly no cellar.

"Dede, I just have to believe this is the house the Lord is providing!" Pat was saying. "Why don't we ask some friends to pray with us about it?"

That same day, back home, Pat got on the phone and prayed with Harald, who was still at his church in Mount Vernon. He also called prayer friends at CBN. After an hour, with Tim following every step, Pat announced that the prayer-answer was unanimous. We could move into the country house.

When the day finally came to leave "B" Street, even I felt a sense of sadness. The three oldest children had their own, individual circle of friends and were understandably sorry to leave them behind. Ann happily toddled around, oblivious to any change.

As we drove away, following the truck in which all our things were piled, the children waved good-by to our little home by the graveyard. The house hadn't been my favorite place in the world but here we were all safe, heading into a new adventure. It might even be an adventure of immense proportions . . . if, by chance, my dream held a message.

By mid-September of that year, 1964, we were living in our plantation mansion. Actually the house wasn't as large as it seemed, as we discovered when we tried to fit our family of six inside its walls, but it was cheerful and comfortable.

Life began to take on a pattern as we adjusted to having no neighbors at all after two years of living on "B" Street with a crush of people and a neighborhood center across the street. Each day Pat would go to the station early and get home late. The children were having a wonderful time exploring every cranny of the old place. Timmy soon learned to track the marshes. He also built a hideaway tree house high up in the magnolia. It immediately became a man's world where he and Gordon escaped their sisters.

During these days it interested me greatly that Pat began talking more and more frequently about "the End Times." We had not spoken in these terms during my Catholic childhood, so I listened carefully as Pat explained to the children that Jesus was going to come back to earth one day, and that his Second Coming would be preceded by a stretch of years known as the End Times. In one sense they would be terrible years, full of earthquakes and wars and famine and lawlessness. But in a deeper sense they would be wonderful years, for it was necessary for them to happen before Jesus came to reign.

Pat felt that the real calling of CBN was to establish a broadcasting network that could strengthen Christians all over the world while there was still time, before the Antichrist who was to come stopped all such voices. This is why he eagerly took every opportunity to expand the network, even though such expansions often required enormous faith. Pat was so sure that CBN had grown out of the mind of Christ that he just knew the Lord would help it to flourish provided only that he and the CBN staff continue to listen, obey and reach out to need.

For Pat, this meant spending his time and energy at a prodigious rate. The children and I developed a life style similar to that of a super-busy corporate executive's family. I learned to grasp even the smallest moment of togetherness.

One hot day in 1965, for example, Pat came home surprisingly early, while Tim and Gordon and Elizabeth were playing "hot box" with two-year-old Ann as the one-woman cheering section. In "hot box" there are two bases and two catchers with mitts and a ball. A third person has to run between the bases without being tagged.

As soon as Pat got out of the car the children began cajoling him to play. "Just one game, Dad," Elizabeth piped up. "Quick, Gordon, throw the ball."

Pat protested, saying he would have to change his suit first. But the kids knew that once Pat walked in the door the phone would ring.

"Come on, Gordon, run after him!" Elizabeth cried. I

couldn't believe my eyes. Pat put down his papers and began to run from base to base. "Watch out, Daddy!" shouted the cheering section. "Hurry up! Hey Elizabeth, hurry up and throw," Gordon yelled.

Well, I figured I had better go out and stop Pat. At least get him to change his brand new suit. But I quickly changed my mind and let Pat have this special moment with the children. In fact I went out myself to watch the game.

I got to the side yard just in time to see Pat trip, get tagged and rip—irreparably rip—his brand new suit. In my mind, I figured if we spent a month economizing we could probably afford another new outfit for Pat. But at that moment I didn't care.

The Lord continued to supply me with unexpected gifts of Himself—perhaps as an encouragement for up-coming times when He knew I would *need* courage?

For weeks I had been dragging around. Was I sick? It was not like me to feel so drained, for I was accustomed to an abundance of energy. I found myself remembering the days back in Queens and again on "B" Street when Pat was so enervated that he could hardly get going in the morning. How I empathized now with the way he must have been feeling. I'd go out to the little catch-all room, where I kept the washer and dryer, intending to get a full load done, then get an early start on dinner. But all I managed was half of my goals.

Then one day when Pat and I were in Miami Beach, Pat asked me to do him a favor. We'd been hearing a lot about a woman named Katherine Kuhlman, but we had never met her.

"Just go listen to her, Honey," Pat suggested one day. "Then tell me what your spirit says."

So I left Pat with the children at our motel and went

to the Deauville where the meetings were being held. The ballroom was jampacked. I was about to take a seat at a table in the rear when I spotted an old friend, Viola Malachuk. Viola had an extra ticket at her up-front table and invited me to join her.

Which is how it happened that I was sitting at the front of the ballroom all during the meeting. I was intrigued with Katherine Kuhlman. She came on a bit dramatically, but there was a sincerity about her that struck me from the very start. At one point Katherine stopped her address and began to look out over the audience, naming specific diseases that were, she said, even then being healed. It was the first time I had seen the "Word of Knowledge" being given freely at a public meeting. I admit that I was a bit doubtful until one woman came into the ballroom carrying a backbrace which she had just taken off in the lady's room. She bent over, twisted her spine, danced, held her brace in the air and called out to everyone, "I've been healed. The Lord's healed me."

Then something else happened. Katherine asked the people who had been touched by God to come forward and she would pray for them. Pray for them? What did she mean? They had already been healed.

People did come forward, though. I watched in interest as they formed a line across the front of the auditorium. For a reason I couldn't fathom, people in the line had someone standing immediately behind them. Katherine walked up to the first person and reached out her hand to touch his forehead. Instantly the man fell backwards. And as he did so, I understood why there were people standing behind the line. They were there to catch people as they fell.

Then I remembered that I had heard of this phenomenon before. Barbara Simmons told me once about a won-

derful experience she called being "slain in the Spirit."*
I remember saying to myself, "You've got to be kidding,
Barbara. Who needs that?"

But now, because people seemed to be getting so much
out of the experience, I found myself wishing with all
my spirit that it would happen to me. How I wanted
Katherine to come by our table.

And that's exactly what happened. Katherine began
to walk through the audience. Everyone was standing
now. Katherine started toward us with her hand raised
slightly. The next thing I knew I was gently falling backwards. Someone caught me. I was stretched out on the
ballroom floor of the Deauville Hotel in Miami Beach,
praying in the Spirit and happier than I have ever known
myself to be.

An hour later I walked to the pool side of our motel
where Pat was playing with the children. I seemed to
be floating, I was so happy. I smiled at everyone I met.

Pat looked at me quizzically. "How'd the meeting go,
Dede?" he asked, drying Ann with a huge beach towel.

"Would you believe it," I said to him, "if someone told
you your wife had been stretched out on the floor of
the Deauville speaking in tongues and thoroughly enjoying herself?"

"No, I *wouldn't* believe it!" Pat said. "What happened?"

The joy of that experience has lasted—not always with
the same intensity, but it has lasted nonetheless, right
up until today.

As major as that event was in my life, something else
took place at the Katherine Kuhlman meeting which I
now believe was also part of God's provision.

One of these days, if we *are* heading into a time of

---

* Later I looked up some Biblical examples of similar experiences.
2 Chronicles 5:13–14; Matthew 28:1–4; Acts 9:4; Acts 26:14.

tribulation, much of the normal worldly provisions may be taken from us. For example, we may no longer have access to doctors and medicines. How will God keep His people healthy during such a day?

Well, after the experience at the Katherine Kuhlman meeting, I think I have an insight into how He might be our supply here too.

Many months after the meeting I once again ran across my friend Viola Malachuk. We began reminiscing about the famous day at the Deauville.

"And how have you been feeling since then?" Viola asked.

"Fine," I said, "never better." It was certainly true. As a nurse I think I would say that I'd experienced a metabolic change that day. Before, I had been dragging around listlessly. Now I was *full* of vitality. I felt good almost all of the time.

"Well, that's the proof of the pudding isn't it?" Viola said.

"Proof of what pudding?"

"You remember . . . " began Viola, and then she told me something I had not known; "when you were lying there on the floor praising God? And Katherine came over and prayed for you? Don't you recall?"

"Not at all." But as Viola was speaking I remembered suddenly how dragged down I had been just before the meeting. I recalled wondering if I were, perhaps, ill. And I recalled that there has been a lot of cancer in the women in our family. "What . . . " I asked Viola, "what did Katherine pray for?"

"Why, Dede," said Viola, still finding it hard to believe that I had been so carried away from this earth that I had not even heard Katherine Kuhlman's words, "Katherine looked right at you and prayed that every bit of cancer would be gone from your body."

So the events of these days were exciting. Being close to nature helped our dispositions enormously. The boys thrived in their new freedom and the girls became intrigued with the land, talking Pat into planting our first garden there in 1966. They worked hard, obeyed all the rules of good gardening, but somehow everything came up infested with worms.

The next season I pitched in too, because I wanted to try my hand at soybeans. We fertilized and prepared the soil and planted rows of tomatoes, corn, kale and carrots . . . and soybeans. The girls' crops did all right, but my poor soys appeared just long enough to let me know that they existed, and then they died.

The farmer from across the way came by and I talked with him about my problem. He said that to grow soybeans, the ground had to be innoculated with soil from a field where soybeans had been grown before. So he helped me to prepare the plot, but our horses broke into the yard and calmly ate my crop! Then a drought got to the beans. And after that there was too *much* rain. The summer my mother died no one tended the garden, and it turned into a weed patch. I always thought I had a green thumb, but where soybeans were concerned, I wasn't doing too well.

With the house, though, I was a bit more successful. Although I was still puzzled about the "missing cellar," and although it took me three years to get around to such essentials as draperies and curtains for all the windows, our house was becoming a pleasant place to live in. Furniture that we were picking up at auctions fit the colonial mood of the drawing room and dining room. The house was easier to keep picked up than our earlier homes because there was so much more space. I could keep the drawing room and dining room neat, then let the rest of the house be more casual. The children enjoyed the house, too, except for one major defect. The water pressure was unbelievable. If I were back on my catch-all porch and turned on the washing machine while someone was showering upstairs, the water simply stopped. Many was the day an angry shout echoed through the old house from some soapy, towel-clad figure standing in the hall upstairs.

"Who's got the water on!"

The veranda at our country house was a special source of joy for me. It was rectangular-shaped and screened in, with a cement floor. My plants did well there, as did my quiet times. We had a table and ladder-back chairs so we could eat out often in the nice weather, looking out over the salt marshes. As Ann grew up, she was always decorating the tables with red and yellow and orange paper flowers.

So things were more or less centered down on the home front, but the Lord was always stretching our faith at CBN. Each time we relaxed from some new venture, two more challenges sprang up. The new challenges often began quite casually. It was just such a casual event that provided a watershed for CBN, growing, interestingly, out of Pat's earlier decision to send $1,000 to Dove Toll for the support of Mrs. Lea in Bolivia. Ever since then CBN had a lively interest in South America and had been helping missions there whenever we could.

One day in May 1967, I went to the studio to see Pat. I could never get used to the sophisticated setup of the new studio. What a contrast to CBN's beginnings! True, the studio was still situated on the edge of Scott's Creek, but not much else was the same. There was a large parking lot filled with late model cars. The building itself had been expanded. It was a fresh, clean looking concrete block and formed-brick structure surrounded by attractive landscaping.

In the reception area people were milling about, some of whom I didn't even know. The barn-like studio was a confusion of heavy cables, cameras, microphones and lights. Behind these were the offices and prayer rooms, and still farther back was Pat's private dressing room.

I knocked and went in. Pat was about to go on camera. There he was in front of his mirror with the makeup girl applying the finishing touches to his pancaked face. Pat grinned at me in the mirror as I stood behind him. He had a letter in his hand which was not unusual, since he used his makeup time to go through the mail.

"Here, Hon, look at this," Pat said, handing me an envelope with its foreign stamp. "I get a feeling in my bones that this is a prophetic message. Just suppose that we are entering the 'End Times.' And just imagine that God wants to tell as many people as possible to be prepared . . ."

As I read the letter my pulse speeded up, for I couldn't help but pick out the words "End Times" in Pat's comment. Why was that?

But Pat was talking excitedly about what appeared to be an ordinary letter. The writer, Sixto Lopez of Bogota, Colombia, was asking Pat if he would like to claim a radio station for the Lord. *That* had a familiar ring!

Pat was speaking again. "Harald and I could go down this fall to check it out. Then if it looks promising, we'll send Henry to Bogota. He can get things rolling."

Pat referred to Henry Harrison who was then managing WXRI. I could see that Pat already had his teeth in this promising situation so I didn't try to stop him. Sure enough, that fall I was saying good-by as Pat flew off on this new venture.

What Pat and Harald enthusiastically described on their return was an up-to-date studio located in a modern office building. But they both came back with a deep concern for the needs they saw in Bogota.

I found myself hearing everything they said as if it might portend things to come. Could Bogota be a symbolic town? It was a city of violence and chaos, along with the strong countermeasures that inevitably follow. Was it a precursor of what we could expect everywhere as healthy societies begin to collapse? Colombia's was a sick economy, too much wealth on one hand, too much poverty on the other. Pat heard one story, which he thought apocryphal, of a missionary who was driving his car through a busy market area, put his arm out the window to signal a turn, and had his watch stolen right off his arm.

"If people are that poor, where is your justice?" I asked. "Isn't there some sort of political answer?"

"I'm sure someone's going to try," Harald said, "but not me. My mandate, and Pat's too, is to preach a change of heart—to rich and poor alike, Dede."

In February 1968, Pat held a telethon called "Nuevo Continente"—"New Continent" for Christ. In one day CBN raised enough money to buy the Bogota station and in just a few weeks I was to have a chance to see for myself the Bogota that Harald and Pat were talking about.

It was Pat's idea to have Tim, who was 13 years old now, go to Bogota for a few weeks. Sixto Lopez arranged for Tim to live with the family of the man from whom we bought the station. In August Pat asked me if I wanted to accompany him to Botota to bring Tim home.

So it was that a few weeks later we were walking through the Bogota airport. Pat and I spotted Tim and Henry and Sixto right away. What a variety! Tim was already close to six feet tall. He stood there smiling, his shock of red hair and his blue eyes a contrast to everyone around him. He looked much older than 13 and so very handsome. Standing next to him was Sixto, short and dark-skinned with straight, shiny black hair. And beside Sixto was our old friend, Henry Harrison, jovial, portly, effervescent as ever.

On the way to our hotel Tim, too, told about the needs of the town. Packs of homeless hungry children were begging in the streets and stealing whatever they could. They slept, Tim said, in doorways, huddled under newspapers for protection against the chill mountain air. Tim's sense of the injustices of life showed when he told about one of Bogota's most famous landmarks, the Gold Museum, which we passed on the way to the hotel. As we drove past the collection of treasures, some of Bogota's poor, dressed literally in rags, shuffled by.

Sixto took us to a hospital run by the Christian and Missionary Alliance Church. The head nurse herself showed us around. Her particular concern, like Tim's, was for the plight of the children of Bogota.

"Oh, you just cannot imagine the needs here," she said as we walked through the hospital halls. "There is never enough food. Children are abandoned every day. If there is any deformity or illness, children are often just turned out. Not because of hardheartedness, but because the extra burden is too much to bear." Pat and I just looked at each other without words.

For the first time I saw the possibility that two major strands in my life might be coming together. One was my "Secret Dream." I felt increasingly that my dream might describe the days before Jesus' return, the days when the world spins toward trouble so fast that it is like an explosion. Parts of the world are already in that troubled time.

Then there is my interest in nutrition. Because during

those troubled days people everywhere will need to know how to get the most value out of the simplest food. I have the strongest desire to teach the Church how to stay energetic and healthy for its work of service when normal food supplies are cut off.

When we got back home a few days later, I had a strange sense that, once having reached this understanding, the Lord was going to unravel the dream which He had given me years ago. The feeling was so strong that one day, for the first time ever, I talked about that dream.

I told Pat.

To my great relief he did not just dismiss the experience. But neither was he very attentive.

"Do you think it was our family in the dream, Dede?" Pat asked, his bushy eyebrows raised in that whimsical way of his.

"I wasn't married at the time. But I know they belonged to me. Yes, I think they were our present family, Pat."

Pat is always interested in looking for Scriptural confirmation of words that seem to come from God. I've admired the way he can so often bring to a conversation, just from his store of knowledge, the Scriptural viewpoint of whatever subject is at hand. He did so now.

"Well, you know, Dede, there is a thread running through the Bible that gives us glimpses of His protection. They show how God provides hiding places for us in troubled times. According to the Bible, we're in for a day of catastrophe, but God protects His own. He hides us in the clefts of rocks, and He has tabernacles prepared for us as a refuge from the storm, and He tells us not to be afraid when the destruction comes. In Revelation especially you get the picture of the throne of God as a safe place where we can dwell, riding just as serene as anything above the storm. It's all good news, because it's saying that while the 'Beast' is roaring, God has prepared protection not destruction for his own people."*

So surprisingly Pat was paying attention to the dream. But then he casually added the obvious thought that had been bothering me all along, too.

"I'm not clear how your dream could be prophetic though, Dede, because there's no cellar in this house."

Which was so obviously true that once again I did what I'd always done; I tucked the dream away.

Not that I forgot it, for it was still just as vivid to me as it had been that night so many years before, when I had no husband or children, when I didn't live in a house in the country with pine trees and a salt marsh. I just tucked this startling dream into a hiding place of its own and said nothing more about it.

Learning to say nothing for a while was something that I believed in more and more. It was part of being submitted. I was certain that a healthy, submitted relationship between husband and wife did *not* mean the wife would become a nothing person. A woman, I just knew, should never experience a submersion of her personality. Scripture tells us to submit, not submerge ourselves.

And, frankly, that distinction had been causing problems. I wasn't sure who I was anymore. People at the station were most cordial, but it was clear, even from my nickname, that I was not really me. I was "Mrs. Pat."

Then one day, quite out of the blue, the matter of my working was in the air again.

A Christian friend called me from one of our local community colleges. She wondered if I would consider com-

---

* Later I looked up some of these references. Exodus 21:13, Isaiah 2:21, Isaiah 4:6, Job 5:20–22.

ing to the school to teach nursing. I was flattered, but I knew that it just wouldn't work because we still had so much station-wagoning to do with the children. I didn't even take the question up with Pat.

But in 1970 this woman called again. She had changed jobs herself and was now working at Tidewater Community College near our home.

"Dede," my friend said, "we want to start a new nursing program. And we would like you to help us set it up. Would you pray about it?"

I promised I would. Ann was in the second grade now; her hours and my hours might mesh. Certainly we needed the money, with four children to put through college.

So one morning I told Pat that I had been asked to go back to work. Pat sat at the kitchen table stirring his tea, but even before he spoke I could tell that his mind was surprisingly receptive because a very slight smile played on the edges of his lips.

Pat, in fact, was delighted. I had not gone out looking for the job, it had come to me which opened the possibility that the offer had come from God. And another thing, he could see as clearly as I could that with his limited salary we really were going to need the money to put the children through school.

So I took the job. Before I left the position eight years later I had become Assistant Professor Adelia Robertson. The work in obstetrical and pediatric nursing was in keeping with all of my training and interest, and I just loved it.

Then one day Pat began to talk about a problem that was emerging at our old house. There was a chimney out back that serviced the oil furnace in the little catch-all room off the kitchen. "That chimney's beginning to crack, Honey," Pat said one morning over his cereal and tea. "It really has to be repaired. What would you think of getting the kitchen remodeled at the same time?"

What a wonderful idea. Even with Tim away at McCallie and with me working again, I still spent a lot of time in the kitchen, and it would be great to have a more functional place in which to work.

So it was that we began to tear down the chimney and to remodel the kitchen and catch-all room into a laundry and sewing room. I deeply suspected that all we were achieving was to transform a small catch-all room into a larger catch-all room, but never mind. It would be a good place for my plants in the wintertime when I couldn't have them out on the veranda.

One day while I was away from home the workmen stumbled onto something interesting. They called Pat at the office and he hurried home.

That day, as I pulled up to the house, Pat met my car.

"Dede, you'll never guess what's happened," Pat said, his eyes bright. He took my hand and started to walk towards the back of the house where a bulldozer was just stopping, its blade resting in a heap of boards and rubble from which dust still rose in a dirty cloud.

"The workmen were knocking out a wall, Sweetheart, and they came to a part of the floor that sounded hollow. They asked me if I'd come home so they could rip it up."

Pat stopped. "Dede . . . " He turned towards me and I knew him well enough to see that he was trying his best to underplay the moment. "Dede, there is an old cellar under this house."

Pat turned again, quickly, and walked toward the place where the workmen had gathered around the back of our home, where their bulldozer had scraped away the old floor.

There, filled with rubble, was the unmistakable outline
of a basement. The foreman kicked aside a brick.

"This may be why the chimney's cracking," the foreman said. "When they filled in that cellar, the rubble
settled. But then . . . "

On and on he went, talking about the structural problems that he was facing, but of course I wasn't listening
to that at all. An eerie sensation came over me. I remembered the day we first came to this house as a family,
when I couldn't get over the feeling that I was walking
through a predestined experience, as if we were supposed
to be in this house for reasons that were not as yet clear.

I didn't need to say anything to Pat, but I was wondering if his flesh was a mass of goose bumps like mine. As
we stood there watching, I found myself remembering
one phrase from Pat's conversation about the way God
provides for His own. Was this another *glimpse of His
protection?*

That afternoon Pat and I took a long walk and spent
a lot of our time talking about the dream. Pat had gone
out on a limb on his television show predicting an atomic
war. Was this dream related to war? Could the dream
be a warning? Could it be that the explosion depicted
warfare that would leave mankind desperately in need
of protection?

We don't know of course. We still don't even know if
the dream is prophetic. It was on that walk that Pat em-
phasized to me how important it is to test prophecy. Test
it against Scripture, test it against the witness of our own
spirit, test it above all by events. We cannot know
whether or not the dream is prophetic until all of it either
comes to pass or does not come to pass.

"The explosion may not even be an atomic disaster,"
Pat said. "It could be just the symbol of some event that

is *like* an explosion because it changes everything. Change is one thing that we're afraid of. Maybe change is going to take place so rapidly that it leaves us feeling devastated."

Well, since that day I have been very anxious to tell people about my dream. That may seem an odd thing to say. Who wants to go through an explosion of any kind, symbolic or literal?

But the real focus of the dream is not on the disaster but on that glimpse of His protection that Pat talks about.

Every time I go down to the newly excavated cellar today, down the four ladder-step stairs, turn right at the landing and go the rest of the way into the basement, I ask myself what should we *do* about the dream?

I am convinced that He wants us to prepare practically. In my dream there was a supply of food and water in the basement, enough to help us through a short period of tribulation. One school of thought is that we should store up food and water, as Joseph stored grain for the time of famine which God told him was to come. If we are to store food, soybeans are an excellent staple; they will keep almost indefinitely and are a near-perfect supply of protein. Over the past few months I've been getting a definite nudge from the Lord to provision our cellar with food. The food I am choosing certainly includes my friend the soybean.

But if we are to be preparing for the End Times in God's way, it is clear to me that a provision of food and water will not be enough. We must be spiritually prepared as well. In fact, there are some Christians who feel that spiritual preparation is the only preparedness worth making. We should store up *spiritual* treasures— with a special emphasis on the Fruit of the Spirit. The treasures of heaven are the power-filled words of God.

With them we are able to move through even the worst
of times, depending on the Lord's own power to take
us through.

So this is why we at CBN have been working so hard.
Our effort has been in the area of strengthening the
Church through evangelism and teaching. After nearly
eight years of teaching at Tidewater I decided to leave
my job to be able to put more of my own efforts behind
this strengthening process. You can't, I decided, solve
people's problems in any ultimate sense except by serving
their inner needs.

CBN has grown dramatically since Pat and I drove out
to the dilapidated building on Scott's Creek:

- CBN is now opening its new headquarters in Vir-
ginia Beach which will house four new studios.
- CBN's staff now numbers more than 800 people.
- CBN opened the doors of its Graduate School of
Communications in the fall of 1978, with 80 students
doing advanced work in this field which has meant
so much to us.
- CBN has two satellite receivers and senders for
communications throughout the world.
- In addition to the nationally televised "700 Club
Program" which Pat hosts, CBN is preparing teaching
shows, news broadcasts and there are plans for a Chris-
tian soap opera and situation comedy.
- There are CBN television programs in nearly all
of the South American countries, in Central America,
Hong Kong, the Philippines, Japan and Africa.
- CBN owns and operates six radio stations in the
United States.
- Eighty-five percent of the homes in America with
TV sets now can view the "700 Club" at least once a
week, and this coverage continues to grow.

• There is a full-time spiritual life director who handles more than 100,000 phone calls each *month* through a chain of prayer counselors around the world.

So we are all working hard to see to it that the spiritual side of our preparation for hard times is well provided for. Pat and I feel that our preparation should be both physical and spiritual. Both approaches are Scriptural. We do approve of people putting aside during a time of plenty for a time of less-than-plenty. And we believe that the material things put aside are to be used in service, not just for ourselves but for the people around us.

But more important is the putting into our hearts the word of God. This is the treasure of heaven that will act as our source of energy and strength and protection during any disaster times.

I have sensed in talking to people about the dream that there is a healthy interest in its meaning. The dream gets us thinking. It leaves us in a positive attitude because one thing is so clear: through the dream we do get a glimpse of His protection.

But beyond that, much is veiled in symbol.

What is its full meaning? Every time I go down into my cellar I wonder at the interpretation.

May I ask an unusual favor? I would really like to hear your interpretation of the dream.

Will you write me? This has been a book about His provision. What is God perhaps providing us through the dream? I'd like to hear what the Lord is whispering in your heart. Just write to:

Dede's Dream
Dede Robertson
CBN Television Network
Virginia Beach, VA 23463

An Exercise in Awareness
of God's Provision

How to put this book to use in your own personal life

ONE MORNING NOT long ago I was standing with Pat in front of Buckingham Palace in London, watching the changing of the guard.

"Imagine!" I said to Pat. "Dede Elmer from Columbus, Ohio, here in front of fabulous Buckingham Palace. What a dream come true."

Later that day I woke up to an interesting fact. The Lord has not only supplied my practical, everyday needs . . . He has *even answered my storybook dreams!* The details were not the same, but the emotions had been satisfied. I dreamed of a glamorous, servant-filled life? Well, many is the time Pat and I have been guests in the most sumptuous, well-staffed homes in the world. Or again: As we were driving for the first time to visit our television station, I fantasized a Hollywood-like TV studio. Well, the new facilities at CBN are among the finest in the world. Again: I dreamed of a life of travel? Pat and I have been to the most exotic spots on earth, all as part of our work.

Why, then, should I ever need to be reminded of His provision?

But I do. Just the other day I found myself confronted with a barrage of facts that attacked my emotions.

In the headlines was the story of still another increase in the price of crude oil; side by side with this article was a story about record inflation. Friends who have a radio ministry had told us just the night before that donations to their work were slowing down. Other friends who own a business, report buyer resistance to higher prices forced by higher costs. Strikes are threatened in two critical industries.

The natural tendency was to be frightened. In the midst of this onslaught I found myself wondering: What can we actually *do* at times like this, when observation and common sense tell us our traditional supply lines are being threatened?

That morning I seemed to hear the Lord say to me, "Dede, one of the reasons for writing this book is to pull together a record of the ways I have always been supplying your every need. Look over your life now and see what you find."

So I took out pen and a pad of paper and began my task.

Material and Physical Needs

OUR SITUATION	GOD'S SUPPLY
(Some of our needs were unimportant, others were major. Both, I found, were emotionally draining at the time.)	(Often coming through "normal" channels but sometimes through mystic means. In both we learn to see the hand of God.)

I want a life companion	I meet and marry Pat
We need training, skills	Pat receives law degree, I a master's degree in nursing
No transportation	Given old car by my parents
We need a place to live	Very nice apartment in Queens
And some extra income	I get a hospital job
Pat loses church position	He is offered work with Harald Bredesen
Our older child, Timmy, ill	God heals him
Food prices rising	I'm reintroduced to soybeans
Pat overtired	Experiences renewed energy through revamping of diet
Week-long radio appearance	Pat is totally at ease
We need money	Mother sends $100
We're swamped by details of house-hunting, job-hunting, launching TV station in Virginia	God provides George Lauderdale
We need a place to stay	God puts us in "prophet's chamber" at Mrs. Jean Mayo's house
No money for advance rent	Contrary to policy, apartment manager waives security requirement

Almost no furniture	We are allowed to rent furniture for $10 a month
Very little money	I find weekend nursing job (and I love it!)
We have far from enough money to buy a TV station	Tim Bright accepts our low offer
Monthly rent continues to strain finances	We're offered rent-free farmhouse
New house needs curtains	The ones I made earlier fit these windows too
The house is pretty empty	Truckload of furniture arrives from my parents
Pat can't run stations, hold down a paying job too	Fred Beasley gives Pat $100 per week for family needs
We have to vacate rent-free house	A second rent-free house made available—and this one close to center where kids can swim!
We long to complete our "dream family"	Ann is born, giving us two boys, two girls: four bright, healthy children!
We wish for own home, more privacy as children grow	We're given gracious colonial home in secluded setting
House needs considerable work	Friends help us paint, do repairs, clean up
We dream of a worldwide Christian communications network	CBN has phenomenal growth, including overseas outreach

I need satisfying work of my own

Am offered teaching job at college level

We've asked God to meet our children's needs as He has met ours

Tim married, studying for ministry

Elizabeth studying business administration

Gordon studying prelaw

Ann in high school, still at home: God knows I'm not quite ready for the empty nest!

Spiritual Needs

Pat and I, like all people, are alienated from God

Pat accepts Jesus' work of reconciliation

I have trouble identifying with the reality of faith

Through Gates of Splendor teaches me that even today people are willing to sacrifice everything for their faith

I want what Pat has found

I accept Jesus at Schroon Lake through ministry of Larry McGuill

Pat needs Christian fellowship

He meets Harald Bredesen, others

I need Christian fellowship too

Christian Women's Club helps me bridge living "in the world" and living for the Lord

Pat needs power and joy in his life	Receives the Baptism in the Holy Spirit
Externally we experience "hard times"	Internally God begins to manifest fruits of the Spirit: love, gentleness, patience
I struggle with self-control	Pat teaches me self-control really means control of self by God
My brother, Ralph, has a crisis	Instead of reacting, I simply flow through it
I fall into habits of negative thinking	God helps me focus on the positive
In the ghetto of Bedford-Stuyvesant we thought *we* were the benefactors!	We realize coming to Bedford-Stuyvesant was primarily for my spiritual benefit
I want the peace, joy I see growing in Pat's life	I receive the Baptism in the Holy Spirit
We're undecided about moving to Virginia	In His mercy, God keeps the future secret, teaches us to move ahead one step at a time
We have $70 with which to buy a TV station	God gives us faith in spite of the figures
We experience material lack	Joy comes not from abundance of things but from total surrender to God's will
We still have few resources	But we now believe God to create something out of nothing

We have to rely for food on gifts from other people

My pride is not wounded; this is the church in action

Kite-flying incident

God shows me my own impatience

I tell Pat about my dream I had in college which begins to come true

Pat helps me look at the dream as part of God's provision

We will be taken to the wilderness again and again

But we have treasures in heaven—especially the power-filled words of God—to help us

We can't possibly be sure of the future

God gives Pat the gift of creative imagination: "walking by faith, not by sight"

We store food and water against a holocaust

But God has shown us that these are to be used in service to those around us. The more important preparation is spiritual

Humanly, I don't want to face a terrifying "end time"

I believe Jesus Himself will see us through

Our household has been through hard times

Through them we are learning to live without anxiety

When I finished this sketchy account of the matching of needs and supply I realized that this is a technique I could use—all of us can use—any time I begin to feel that we may be in short supply, either physically or spiritually. God has been providing us with a steady harvest of the Fruit of the Spirit over the years.

And I am confident at the deepest level that He is going to continue doing so.

The next time you yourself feel the familiar tug of fear, get out this book and review with me how God has been providing for one ordinary family.

Then make your own "Exercise in God's Provision."

In one column write what your needs have been for, say, the last year in your life. In another column write God's provisions, as I have done. Make similar listings of your spiritual needs and His provisions.

Next, make copies of these lists. You may want to keep one by your telephone or on your dressing table, or wherever you're apt to think about your needs and start feeling blue. Of course a list 1,000 pages long could never include all of God's provisions! We'd have to start with Jesus Himself, with life itself, with air to breathe and an earth to inhabit, the thousand chemical balances continually correcting themselves in our bodies, speech, memory, and so on. Our lists represent only a fraction of His constant care.

But the value of our list is that it is specific. As it builds, one provision on top of the other, our faith is being restored. God has provided our needs.

We can rejoice in His supply.

And in the fact that He is not suddenly going to change His nature.